Routledge Revivals

The Story of Meriadoc, King of Cambria

The Story of Meriadoc, King of Cambria
(Historia Meriadoci, Regis Cambrie)

Volume 50
Series A
Garland Library of Medieval Literature

Edited and Translated by
Mildred Leake Day

First published in 1988 by Garland Publishing, Inc.

This edition first published in 2019 by Routledge
2 Park Square, Milton Park, Abingdon, Oxon, OX14 4RN
and by Routledge
52 Vanderbilt Avenue, New York, NY 10017, USA

Routledge is an imprint of the Taylor & Francis Group, an informa business

© 1988 by Mildred Leake Day

All rights reserved. No part of this book may be reprinted or reproduced or utilised in any form or by any electronic, mechanical, or other means, now known or hereafter invented, including photocopying and recording, or in any information storage or retrieval system, without permission in writing from the publishers.

Publisher's Note
The publisher has gone to great lengths to ensure the quality of this reprint but points out that some imperfections in the original copies may be apparent.

Disclaimer
The publisher has made every effort to trace copyright holders and welcomes correspondence from those they have been unable to contact.
A Library of Congress record exists under ISBN:

ISBN 13: 978-0-367-19527-4 (hbk)
ISBN 13: 978-0-367-19528-1 (pbk)
ISBN 13: 978-0-429-20294-0 (ebk)

The Garland Library of Medieval Literature

General Editors
James J. Wilhelm, Rutgers University
Lowry Nelson, Jr., Yale University

Literary Advisors
Ingeborg Glier, Yale University
William W. Kibler, University of Texas
Norris J. Lacy, University of Washington
Giuseppe Mazzotta, Yale University
Fred C. Robinson, Yale University
Aldo Scaglione, University of North Carolina

Art Advisor
Elizabeth Parker McLachlan, Rutgers University

Music Advisor
Hendrik van der Werf, Eastman School of Music

The Story of Meriadoc, King of Cambria (Historia Meriadoci, Regis Cambrie)

edited and translated by
MILDRED LEAKE DAY

Volume 50
Series A
GARLAND LIBRARY OF MEDIEVAL LITERATURE

Garland Publishing, Inc.
New York and London
1988

© 1988 Mildred Leake Day
All rights reserved

LIBRARY OF CONGRESS
Library of Congress Cataloging-in-Publication Data

Historia Meriadoci, Regis Cambrie. English.
 The Story of Meriadoc, King of Cambria = Historia Meriadoci, Regis Cambrie / edited and translated by Mildred Leake Day.
  p. cm. — (Garland library of medieval literature ; v. 50. Series A)
 Translation of: Historia Meriadoci, Regis Cambrie.
 Bibliography: p.
 ISBN 0-8240-8479-9
 1. Meriadoc (Legendary character)—Romances. 2. Arthurian romances. 3. Romances, Latin (Medieval and modern)—Translations into English. 4. Romances, English—Translations from Latin (Medieval and modern). I. Day, Mildred Leake, 1929–   II. Title. III. Series: Garland library of medieval literature ; v. 50.
 PA8330.H75E5   1988
 821'.1—dc19   88-24399
                                                                  CIP

Printed on acid-free, 250-year-life paper
Manufactured in the United States of America

For all my family

my parents Howard and Marjory Leake

my sons and daughters, their husbands and wives

Marjory and Nelson Cooper, Jim and Cynthia Day,

Susan and Karl Kling, Howard and Sharon Day

Roger and Jodie Day

my grandchildren

Crystal Day, Wesley Day, Sarah Cooper, David Kling

and my husband Jim

Preface of the General Editors

The Garland Library of Medieval Literature was established to make available to the general reader modern translations of texts in editions that conform to the highest academic standards. All of the translations are originals, and were created especially for this series. The translations attempt to render the foreign works in a natural idiom that remains faithful to the originals.

The Library is divided into two sections: Series A, texts and translations; and Series B, translations alone. Those volumes containing texts have been prepared after consultation of the major previous editions and manuscripts. The aim in the editing has been to offer a reliable text with a minimum of editorial intervention. Significant variants accompany the original, and important problems are discussed in the Textual Notes. Volumes without texts contain translations based on the most scholarly texts available, which have been updated in terms of recent scholarship.

Most volumes contain Introductions with the following features: (1) a biography of the author or a discussion of the problem of authorship, with any pertinent historical or legendary information; (2) an objective discussion of the literary style of the original, emphasizing any individual features; (3) a consideration of sources for the work and its influence; and (4) a statement of the editorial policy for each edition and translation. There is also a Select Bibliography, which emphasizes recent criticism on the works. Critical writings are often accompanied by brief descriptions of their importance. Selective glossaries, indices, and footnotes are included where appropriate.

The Library covers a broad range of linguistic areas, including all of the major European languages. All of the important literary forms and genres are considered, sometimes in anthologies or selections.

The General Editors hope that these volumes will bring the general reader a closer awareness of a richly diversified area that has for too long been closed to everyone except those with precise academic training, an area that is well worth study and reflection.

James J. Wilhelm
Rutgers University

Lowry Nelson, Jr.
Yale University

Contents

Introduction	xiii
Select Bibliography	li
The Story of Meriadoc, King of Cambria	1

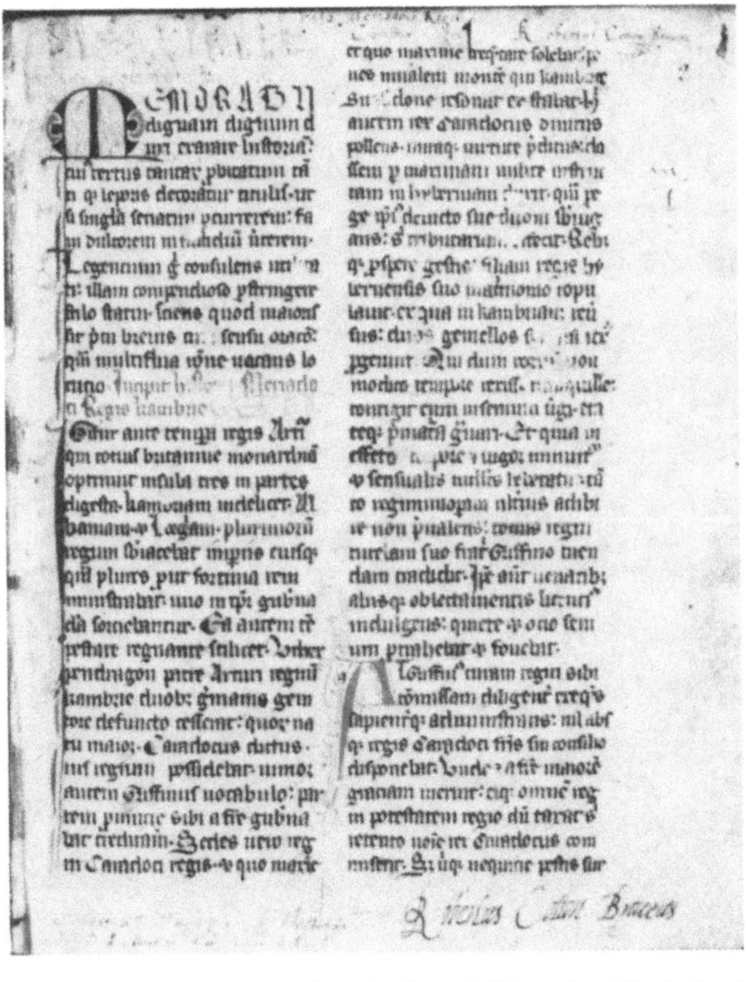

Plate 1. The opening folio of *Historia Meriadoci Regis Cambrie* in British Library Cotton Faustina B vi, f.1. (Reproduced by permission of the British Library.)

INTRODUCTION

Date and Authorship

Historia Meriadoci regis Cambrie, "The Story of Meriadoc, King of Cambria" is about a prince of the kingdom of Cambria (pre-Saxon Wales) who, after surviving an attempted assassination by his uncle, fights as a young knight in the cause of royal justice. With Arthur's help he brings his usurping uncle to trial for the murder of his father. As Arthur's champion in three judicial duels, he not only defeats the contending knights, but he acts to prevent Arthur from unjust acquisition of their land. Then, laying aside his reign in Cambria in favor of his twin sister and her husband King Urien, he takes the position of a mercenary in the service of the Emperor of the Alemanni in order to bring peace to the warring realms of Europe — for war is no more than a judicial duel between kings and, like the judicial duels fought in Arthur's court, not a system of justice but a contest of power. But Meriadoc is compromised by his position as a mercenary, and although he defeats the King of the Land From Which No One Returns and rescues the Emperor's only daughter, he falls victim to the Emperor's political necessity. In the end, he must act on his own in the cause of justice; and it is the Emperor's enemy, the King of Gaul, who finally grants Meriadoc his just reward.

Historia Meriadoci Regis Cambrie (hereafter *Meriadoc*) has survived in two manuscripts, British Library Cotton Faustina B VI, ff. 1r-23r, and Bodleian Rawlinson B 149, pp. 91-132. Following *Meriadoc* in the Cotton manuscript is a second romance *De ortu Waluuanii*, "The Rise of Gawain," which scholars agree is by the same author (Bruce, 1913, pp. vii-x; Rajna, 1927; Loomis, 1959, p.

473. References are to the Select Bibliography). The Latin style and vocabulary are similar, as is the author's treatment of the Arthurian material. For example, in both romances Kay is Arthur's honored seneschal, and Arthur, although treated with respect, is the one who gets humbled by the young hero.

Although *Meriadoc* was composed in prose rather than verse, it is not a late romance. The earlier manuscript, British Museum Cotton Faustina B vi, is written in a hand of the first quarter of the fourteenth century, but the date of the original composition is debated. J. D. Bruce suggests the second quarter of the thirteenth century (1913, pp. xvi–xxiv). R. S. Loomis proposes an even later date, after 1277, because he sees a similarity between Arthur's campaign against Griffin and the historical campaign of Edward I against Llewelyn, the last native prince of Wales, who was besieged at Mount Snowdon in 1277 and forced to surrender (1959, pp. 473–474). Yet details of armor, costume, and ship construction in *De ortu Waluuanni* suggest composition in the late twelfth century, as does the concern in *Meriadoc* over the legitimacy of the judicial duel and the role of the mercenary knight.

The judicial duel as a legal procedure for settling property disputes was an established custom. The wager of battle was accepted as proof of God's will in the absence of other proof. The procedure of the judicial duel was performed before legal witnesses and followed a set format. The litigants could do battle in person or appoint champions. The outcome was accepted as revealing God's justice, as in the confrontation between David and Goliath. The judicial duel seems to have been a generally accepted legal procedure throughout most of Europe. It was pre-Christian among the Irish Celts, appearing in the *Senchus More*, a code traditionally compiled under the supervision of St. Patrick. The Welsh laws attributed to Hoel Dda (early tenth century) give details of proper procedure. The Danish historian Saxo Grammaticus suggests that the custom originated for the Danes during the reign of Frotho III at the beginning of the Christian era (Lea, pp. 101–117).

Introduction

Opposition to the judicial duel, however, began as early as the eleventh century and becomes well-documented in the twelfth (Lea, pp. 199-206). In 1179 Henry II offered a trial by a jury of twelve knights as an alternative to the judicial duel in property disputes (Warren, p. 352). The Church was active throughout this period trying to discredit the duel, an effort that culminated under Innocent III in the Lateran Council of 1215 (Lea, pp. 206-208). Althought it is not possible to establish a firm date for the composition of *Meriadoc* based on the clear disapproval of the judicial duel in the text, a date of composition in the period of Henry II's innovations in property law and before the absolute condemnation of the Lateran Council might be considered.

The author of *Meriadoc* treats Meriadoc's choice of serving the Emperor as a mercenary as a noble ambition. Such an attitude toward mercenaries did not hold into the mid-thirteenth century. J. F. Verbruggen, in *The Art of Warfare in Western Europe during the Middle Ages*, explains that the role of the mercenary knight in the twelfth and thirteenth centuries reveals first a pattern of increasing importance, particularly notable with King Stephen, who made successful use of Flemish mercenaries led by William of Ypres. But following the rampaging of undisciplined groups of mercenaries, the Church forbade the employment of certain of these, charging brutality, at the Third Lateran Council of 1179. Nevertheless, the use of paid troops was continued by Henry II, Frederick Barbarossa, the sons of Henry II, and Philip Augustus. Richard the Lion-Hearted used Welsh, Genoese, *Brabantiones*, and Saracens, men recruited for their military skills and commanded by the famous Mercadier. Philip Augustus, fighting against Richard, employed a mercenary leader named Cadoc, who remained in the royal service. Yet Cadoc's career declined, and after 1220 he spent six years in prison for a variety of misdeeds. Meanwhile, King John, unable to count on the military assistance of the English nobility, made extensive use of mercenaries, so much so that they became one of the issues addressed in the Magna Carta, where the king was required to send away "all

foreign knights and crossbowmen and mercenaries who had crossed over with their arms and horses to harm the land." This is addressed in Clauses 50 and 51 of the Charter of 1215 (pp. 117–125).

The author of *Meriadoc* makes a case against the judicial duel as well as dramatizing the ambiguity of the role of a nobleman enlisted as a mercenary. In the twelfth century these would have been active concerns for the author and his audience; in the thirteenth century less so. If the work was written at the time suggested by Bruce (second quarter of the thirteenth century) or Loomis (fourth quarter of the thirteenth century), the narrative tension developed by the relevance of these issues would no longer exist.

The armor in *Meriadoc* is also more appropriate to the twelfth than to the thirteenth century. The single detail of armor in the story is the helmet with a nasal piece to protect the face that the Black Knight is wearing at the duel at the ford. Helmets with nasals went out of general use for head protection toward the end of the twelfth century as the superior protection of the "pot" helmet became apparent (Smail, 107). However, that detail by itself cannot be relied on to establish a twelfth–century date. Arthurian knights sometimes wore helmets with nasals in versions of the legend known to have been written in the thirteenth century (Bruce, 1913, pp. xix–xxi).

De ortu Waluuanii, written by the same anonymous author, offers further material to consider in proposing a late twelfth–century date for the composition of *Meriadoc* (Day, 1984, xiii–xxvii). First, the young Waluuanius (Gawain) is called "The Knight of the Surcoat." The surcoat for armor comes into use in the twelfth century, suggesting a period for the costume to be distinctive enough to become a nickname for a knight. Second, the ship construction as noted in the narrative represents twelfth–century engineering. The forecastle and aftercastle are added after the ship is already constructed, and the ram is an essential part of the offensive armor of the vessel. Third, Greek

fire, which is described at length as the ultimate challenge for Gawain, is a weapon of terror for the twelfth century. In the thirteenth, the use of Greek fire had become more common, and knowledge of its limitations had somewhat reduced its emotional value. Fourth, the primary quest for Gawain suggests the historical concern of the Crusaders of the last quarter of the twelfth century. Gawain is sent to relieve the siege of Jerusalem, not to recapture it. Jerusalem, which was in the possession of the Franks from 1099, was taken by Saladin in 1187, never to be regained. Gawain's great duel that restores peace to the beleaguered city is more appropriate to a date before Saladin's victory than after it. As with the judicial duel and role of mercenary in *Meriadoc*, these elements of *De ortu Waluuanii* would have constituted a narrative of immediate relevancy in the twelfth century but would have been somewhat out-of-date for the thirteenth.

If a date for *Meriadoc* seems elusive, the author is even more so. The manuscript gives no indication of its author other than the initial "R" on the opening line, folio 1r: "Incipit prologus R." The only name attributed to *Meriadoc* and *De ortu Waluuanii* is that of Robert of Torigni, abbot of Mont St. Michel from 1154 to 1186, but the possibility of his authorship has not been accepted by Bruce, Loomis, and others. Robert's name is first connected with the Latin romances in the catalog of monastic libraries compiled by John Bale in the sixteenth century (Morriss, pp. 599–645). Bale notes that "Gesta Maradoci (li.l. 'Memoratu dignam')" along with "Gesta Walwani" were listed as works of Robert of Mont St. Michel "ex Nordouencensi Scriptorum catalogo." The ascription of these works to Robert as found in the catalog of the Norwich Library is recorded in Bale's autograph notebook. Bale subsequently used this information in compiling the list of Robert's works in *Scriptorum Illustrium Maioris Britannie...Catalogus*, published in 1557 (II, 131-132). Bale's autograph notebook was first published in 1902 under the title *Index Britanniae Scriptorum*.

Robert's career was exemplary as an abbot and a scholar. His name first appears in 1128 when he enrolled in the Benedictine monastery and school at Bec in Normandy. In 1139 he was the monastery librarian. In 1154 Henry II concurred to Robert's election as abbot of Mont St. Michel, a religious position of considerable esteem. Robert's term of office was a strong one in the history of the abbey. The number of resident monks doubled; major rebuilding was accomplished; its reputation for learning in the classics and the sciences—medicine, astronomy, music—was wide-spread. The abbey was host to Henry II on a number of occasions. Once in 1158 both King Henry and King Louis VII were guests. Abbey business also required Robert to travel to England (Gout, I, 141-155).

While Robert's seventeenth-century biographer, Dom Jean Huynes, records an extravagant tradition that Robert wrote 140 books, the list of his extant known writings is still impressive (Howlett, p. xvi): 1. Additions to the *Chronicle* of William of Jumièges, including the eighth book in its entirety. 2. *Roberti Accessiones ad Sigebertum* (Robert's *Chronicle*). 3. *Chronicon Beccense*. 4. *Continuatio Beccensis*. 5. *Annals of Mont St. Michel, 1135-1173*. 6. *Rubrica Abbreviata*. 7. The prologue to an edition of Pliny's *Natural History*. 8. The prologue to a collection of extracts from St. Augustine which he discovered to have been wrongly attributed to Bede. 9. The *Catalog* of the library at Bec. Of these works, the best known is his *Chronicle*, which was organized as a continuation of the universal history of Sigebert of Gembloux, covering the events of the reigns of Stephen and Henry II and including, like Sigebert, the events of other kingdoms, ranging as far as Jerusalem.

Robert is considered a major historian of his period, yet Robert's name is also associated with romance and with the Arthurian material. In 1139 during the time he was librarian at Bec, Robert was responsible for showing a copy of Geoffrey of Monmouth's *Historia Regum Britanniae* to Henry of Huntingdon. Henry of Huntingdon relates the incident, the earliest recorded

Introduction

mention of Geoffrey's work, in his introductory remarks for "Letter to Warinus," a summary of the *Historia* (Delisle, I, 97–119). Robert's one other recorded connection with romance is in "Le Roman du Mont–Saint–Michel," where the poet–monk William of Sainte Paire tells how he wrote it during the time Robert was abbot (Howlett, p. ix; Adams, p. 12). But no mention of Robert as the actual author of any romances has survived. Nevertheless his influence on Arthurian romance is significant: he included Henry of Huntingdon's "Letter to Warinus" in the preface to his *Chronicle*, and chroniclers who drew on his *Chronicle* gradually incorporated that separate material into the historical records of the early Middle Ages. Henry of Huntingdon's summary in Robert's *Chronicle* is the link between Geoffrey of Monmouth's account of the kings of Britain and subsequent historical works.

Bruce, unaware of Bale's citation of Robert of Torigni as author when he edited *De ortu Waluuanii* in 1898 and *Meriadoc* in 1900, had proposed as the author an unknown English clerk of the thirteenth century living in the southwest of England. Even after 1908 when Margaret Shove Morriss had drawn scholarly attention to Bale's citation, Bruce, in both his 1913 editions and in *The Evolution of Arthurian Romance*, 1923, persisted in his original theory of unknown authorship, and most scholars followed him, rejecting Robert's authorship because of the early date required and because of the difference in style between his known historical writing and the romances.

Meanwhile a few scholars did consider the twelfth–century date and Robert's possible authorship. R. Zenker (pp. 14, 106) and Alfons Hilka (pp. 82–83) discuss the Latin romances as possibly written in the twelfth century. It is interesting that in the margin of the copy of Alfons Hilka's essay in the *Kritischer Jahresbericht* (p. 82) in the library at the University of Tennessee there is a note in the margin in Bruce's hand: "See my new edition of these romances (Göttingen 1913) in which Miss Morriss's dating of these works is disproved."

After the publication of Bruce's editions of 1913, Pio Rajna wrote two papers on *De ortu Waluuanii* and *Meriadoc*. The first (1927) explores in detail the style of the two romances, affirming that they are by the same author. Rajna cites as confirmation the entry by Bale from the Norwich catalog on Robert as the author of the two romances. The second (1930) was published posthumously and unfinished, but the work records Rajna's exploration of what the acceptance of Robert as author would mean to the position of the Latin romances within the framework of the development of Arthurian literature.

Other scholars who followed Bruce in rejecting the authorship of Robert created their own assessment of the author from indications in the text. All agree that the author was well-educated because of his fluent Latin and classical references. Ernst Brugger argues that he was a Welshman (p. 439). William Mullen points out clerical opposition to Arthur as evidenced in various saints' lives and concludes that the author of these two secular romances would probably not have been a monk. He suggests an Englishman or Anglo-Norman writing about 1200 (pp. 58–71). Loomis says, "Presumably then, he was a cleric of English or Norman blood, who lived on the marches of South Wales about 1280" (1959, p. 474). James Wieber agrees with Loomis (pp. 6–22), as does Aubrey Galyon (p. 340).

A working hypothesis concerning date and authorship is essential in order to reach a conclusion about where the Latin romances fit in the context of other Arthurian material. Bruce was defending his thesis that all Arthurian romances stem from the work of the great early French poets. So for him, a French rhymed original must have existed, influenced by Chrétien, that the Latin author later translated. Therefore he assumed a thirteenth-century date of composition as necessary. The rest of his research on dating was a reinforcement of this assumption. Yet no compelling need exists to label a romance written in Latin in either the twelfth or thirteenth century as a "working up" of written French sources, as Bruce insists, or as a "rhetorical

exercise," as Loomis terms it. Original Latin literature of all kinds, poetry and prose, was being composed during this period, particularly in the twelfth century. A broad international audience for Latin literature existed in the monasteries, the universities, and also in the royal courts. Henry II is remembered for being "literatus," fluent in Latin.

Meriadoc and *De ortu Waluuanii* share the commonplaces of episode and detail familiar from the great body of Arthurian literature, but they are not as directly dependent on Chrétien as they are on Geoffrey of Monmouth. *De ortu Waluuanii*, for example, is in some details more primitive than might be expected of a translation of a late twelfth or early thirteenth-century French romance. Rajna notes the primitive quality of Arthur's court, where horses can be brought into the royal sleeping chamber or an envoy from Rome can be received by the King, holding court outside under an ash tree. Rajna also points out that Kay lacks the rudeness of the developed French tradition, Arthur's queen is a sorceress named Guendoloena (a name and characterization not found elsewhere), and Arthur himself is a fighting king, proud of being without a peer among his own knights (1930, pp. 243–244).

Meriadoc shares many of these aspects. The character of Kay the Seneschal is not like the Kay of the French romances. Even though Meriadoc first encounters Kay as the armored knight who abducts him from the forest where he and Orwen have been hidden by the huntsman Ivor, Meriadoc holds no resentment toward Kay, nor do any of Kay's subsequent actions merit it. In fact, Kay assists Meriadoc with the recognition of Ivor at Arthur's court. It is Kay who knights Meriadoc. So when Kay must fight the Black Knight, Meriadoc steps in to take his place and save him the possible shame of defeat. The Kay of the Latin romances is the positive character of the Kay of Geoffrey (Gowans, pp. 44–45). Other details suggest composition before the major developments in the Arthurian legend. Lancelot is not among Arthur's knights. When Arthur's forty best knights must fight the Black Knight, a "line-up" of knights in order of rank is given. The three highest

are Kay, Gawain, and Arthur. Gawain remains the top-ranked fighting man in *Meriadoc*, while the King himself would have taken the final position in the judicial duel.

Still nothing proves a date of composition. There may have been an older tale from which *Meriadoc* was taken, as the author "R" says in his prologue. Whether it was oral or written and which language was used, he does not say. Some of the folklore that the tale encompasses, Germanic as well Celtic, is ancient. The turning of the material into its Latin form may have happened as early as the beginnings of romance in the later twelfth century, or it may have been done at any time between then and the date of the older manuscript copy, early fourteenth century.

So also the author remains elusive but for his initial "R." What can we say about him from the text? With his material combining Celtic and Germanic folklore, he might be English or he might be Norman. The man we are searching for has a bent not only for literature but for law, engineering, and history. He seems to write for an equally educated audience, and he may be connected to a court or major abbey. The concerns with law and with the role of mercenary knight seem to reflect late twelfth-century interests. Such a time frame would fall barely within the later years of Robert of Torigni. But that is not proof of authorship. Even the catalog at Norwich that Bale saw only records what the librarian had noted about the author of the romances. The best we can say is that the author of *De ortu Waluuanii* and *Meriadoc* was a man very much like Robert, whom Henry II appointed as abbot of Mont St. Michel in 1154.

Sources and Influence

Although Bruce postulated a French rhymed source for *Meriadoc*, none has yet been found. The 'Meriadeuc' of French romance (*Le Chevalier aux deux Epées*, French verse, early thirteenth century), is a different character and his adventures are not the same. Meriadeuc's father was killed in battle by Gawain, and Meriadeuc's quest is for revenge. The sources of a few phrases in *Meriadoc* can be identified from Geoffrey of Monmouth and Virgil. The names of three characters and a suggestion for the final battle came from French history, probably Gregory of Tours' *Historia Francorum*. Beyond these, a source study for *Meriadoc* must rely on folkloric analogues, and these, in contrast to the bulk of the Arthurian legend, include Germanic folklore with the Celtic. The folkloric analogues may be best approached, first, with the structure of the work as a whole, then with individual episodes. A few analogues are close enough to suggest the possibility of direct influence by *Meriadoc* on two later romances, *The Awntyrs off Arthure at the Terne Wathelyne* and Malory's "Tale of Gareth."

The plot of *Meriadoc* follows the outline of the hero tale as defined by Otto Rank and others. Meriadoc is of noble birth, but he experiences an endangered childhood. He is raised in a simple, primitive environment. When he reaches adulthood, he takes revenge on the man who caused his exile. He then goes forth into the world and wins a bride and a kingdom.

More specifically, *Meriadoc* is related to a particular group of tales comprising a variation of the hero tale known as "The Widow's Son's Vengeance," a pattern identified by Jean-Claude Lozac'hmeur from his study of the structure of the hero tale in *Perceval* and its analogues. Perceiving the variation as an initiatory myth, Lozac'hmeur compares versions of the myth in a number of cultures and languages. He points out eleven shared features: 1. An oracle announcing the death of the king. 2. Imprisonment of the princess. 3. Seduction of the princess. 4. Murder of the father.

5. Flight of the widow. 6. Rustic childhood of the hero. 7. Discovery of the identity of the murderer. 8. Challenge of the usurper. 9. Tests imposed on the hero. 10. Punishment of the murderer. 11. The hero becomes king (pp. 45–63).

The plot of *Meriadoc* contains features 1, 4, 6, 7, 8, 9, 10, and 11. Since the widow dies of a broken heart immediately after the murder, "5. The flight" is carried out by the foster parents with the children. Meriadoc's sister, not his mother, is the victim of "2. Seduction of the princess," with the crisis of the princess following "6, The rustic childhood."

Yet a consideration of the final episodes shows that *Meriadoc* does not exactly follow the pattern as outlined. The traditional hero tale has a "there and back again" structure, a cycle that shows the hero replacing his father. Meriadoc, although taking revenge on his evil uncle, does not return home to replace his father. Instead, he takes a bride in another kingdom and remains there to rule. The pattern can be considered cyclical only if one assumes a matrilineal concept of kingship: a prince must win his bride and occupy the throne that she inherits. That such a pattern may have shaped the folklore upon which *Meriadoc* is based is also indicated by the decision of Meriadoc to leave the kingdom of Cambria with his sister and her husband and go off to seek adventure. On the other hand, the author himself may have so shaped the plot in order to bring his hero to the continent to fight in the final battle between the Emperor of the Alemanni and the King of Gaul, an engagement that is possibly a romanticized version of the decisive battle of Tolbiac (c. 496 or 506 A. D.) between the Alemanni and Clovis, King of the Franks, who as victor over Syagrius (c. 486) was King of Gaul as well (Van de Vyver, pp. 793–813).

Several critics have developed the comparative analogues of individual episodes in *Meriadoc*, primarily Max Deutschbein, J. D. Bruce, Oscar L. Olson, R. S. Loomis, and William Mullen. Mullen divides the episodes into five groups: the *Enfances* of Meriadoc, the Combat at the Ford, the Faery Mistress, The Perilous Castle, and the Abduction (pp. 5–57). These analogues will be

Introduction

summarized; other analogues which they did not note I will present in greater detail.

In the opening episode of the *Enfances*, King Caradoc of Cambria is assassinated by his brother Griffin. Bruce has examined this material and found no parallel in either Welsh history, the romances written about Carados Brie-Bras, or the *Mabinogion* (1913, pp. xxvi-xxvii). However in the *Mabinogion*, "Branwen daughter of Llyr," there is a Caradawg son of Bran whose death is caused by his kinsman Caswallawn son of Beli (Ford, pp. 70-71). "Branwen" would not be considered a source for *Meriadoc*, but the bitter relationship between Wales and Ireland, the attempted union by a treaty of marriage, the sacrifice of the half-Welsh, half-Irish princeling, the death of the bride of a broken heart, and the treacherous accession to the kingship of Britain by Caswallawn may have been part of the folkore that shaped the Welsh flavor of the *Enfances*.

Other analogues to the endangered childhood of Meriadoc are clearly Germanic. First identified by Max Deutschbein in 1906 and elaborated by Oscar Ludvig Olson in 1916, the story of the attempted murder of Meriadoc and Orwen has parallels in the *Havelock* tales. Elements of plot appear in Gaimar's *Estoire des Engleis* (1145-1151), the *Lai d'Haveloc* (late twelfth century), and the English *Havelok* (later thirteenth century). Another analogue is the Hroar-Helgi story found in *Hrolfssaga* (fourteenth century) and in Saxo Grammaticus, *Gesta Danorum* (late twelfth or early thirteeth century). In these stories the young heirs are ordered slain by the usurping monarchs but are rescued by humble people. Eventually they discover their royal lineage and exact vengeance, regaining their rightful inheritance (Mullen, pp. 5-18). The relationship between the *Havelock* analogues and *Meriadoc* is reinforced by names. "Orwen" appears in *Meriadoc* as the name of the twin sister, and in Gaimar's *Havelok*, "Orwen" is the name of the mother of the bride Argentille. The related name "Ogn" appears as the name of the bride of Hroar, hero of the *Hrolfssaga* version (Bruce, 1913, p. xxvii, note 1). The curious emanation of

royalty that identifies Havelock is also described for Meriadoc and Orwen, "from them something more than mortal shone forth" (p. 27). Deutschbein concludes that the *Enfances* of Meriadoc represent a Welsh version of the Havelock legend, demonstrating the movement of a traditional tale from the sagas brought by the Danes to England into the body of Welsh story material. He characterizes the motif as "exile/revenge."

Oscar Olson develops the parallels from Danish and Icelandic materials in more detail. He notes that Saxo Grammaticus, Book 7, relates the history of brothers who are joint kings: Frothi and Halfdan. Frothi secretly plots the murder of Halfdan and then attempts to eliminate Halfdan's two sons as well. But their guardians fake evidence of an attack by wolves and, with the bodies of slaves' children slain in their stead, claim that the princes have perished. Meanwhile the two princes are hidden in a hollow oak tree, where food is brought to them under the pretense that they are dogs. Even the names of hounds are given to them. Later when the two become young men, they take vengeance on their father's slayer by burning down his hall. In fact, Olson proposes *Meriadoc* as influencing Saxo for two verbal echoes: first, Ivor and his wife and dog hide in an "ilex", or holly-oak, as do the boys using the dogs' names in Saxo; second, the Latin words "fumique vapore", describing Ivor's effort to smoke out the executioners, appear at the end of the same tale in Saxo when the two princes set fire to the hall of their evil uncle, and he perishes "strangulatus vapore et fumo" (pp. 74-76).

The *Havelock* motif appears in at least one other Arthurian romance. In the early part of the Prose *Lancelot*, the two orphaned children of King Bors are in mortal danger from King Claudas. They are saved by being magically transformed into dogs. However, there does not seem to be any direct influence of this variant on *Meriadoc*. The *Meriadoc* and the Prose *Lancelot* episodes have less in common with each other than either does with the saga versions.

Introduction

But while earlier scholars have suggested that the traditions of the Danes of England may be the source of the *Meriadoc* episode, the evidence of a variant in the Prose *Lancelot* suggests that the circulation and influence of the *Havelock* tales is complex. A major difference between the story material in *Meriadoc* and the variants in the *Havelock* tales is in the elaborate cruelty of the fate ordered by Griffin for his brother's children. The deaths of a ten-year-old boy and his twin sister could have been accomplished much more simply than the elaborate routine the story relates — as in the proposed drowning of Havelock. Although the author does not specifically say that the prince and princess in *Meriadoc* are condemned to a ritual sacrifice rather than to a particularly cruel assassination, the folklore source may have offered such a description. In *Meriadoc*, twelve executioners are sworn to the task, the children are to be taken from the king's court at Snowdon to Arglud (possibly Dumbarton on the Clyde), hanged from an ancient oak tree "growing there since the flood," and slaughtered.

The oak described in *Meriadoc* is no common forest tree. Its trunk is so huge that the twelve agents of the king can take refuge in its hollow. The location of the tree is in what the author calls a "nemus," the Latin term for an open place in a forest, sometimes a sacred grove. The term is best known from the Lake of Nemi, location of the sacred grove of Diana Nemorensis of classical mythology, the setting for the basic myth of Sir James Frazer's *The Golden Bough* (pp. 3–7). Griffin's instructions for the slaying of the children share significant details with the description of the ritual sacrifice made by Robert Graves in *The White Goddess*. Graves, who seems not to have been familiar with *Meriadoc*, collated the grisly details of the ritual death of Hercules from many sources, noting the presence of twelve "merry men" who hang the victim from an oak and then dismember him, throwing the bloody remains into the fires prepared for the purpose (pp. 125–126).

In fact, the details of the entire episode, from the murder of Caradoc by his brother in a "hunting accident" until the escape of Ivor with the children, can be related to material gathered by Frazer to support his theory of ritual kingship in *The Golden Bough*. Frazer uses the Greek myth of King Athamus as one example. The myth relates how King Athamus tried to sacrifice his son and daughter for the fertility of the land, but they were saved by Zeus, who took the form of a ram with golden fleece and carried them away. Later an oracle required the death of King Athamas, but he went mad and "mistaking his son Learchus for a wild beast shot him dead" (pp. 243–244). Robert Graves, in *The Greek Myths* lists many versions and fragments of this tale: Herodotus, Pausanias, Apollodorus, Hyginus, Sophocles, Euripides, Ovid. Graves' summary adds the presence of dogs and wolves with the sheep in some versions (I, 225–231). Herodotus includes the myth in his *History* as an example of a cult of sacrificial kingship that impressed Xerxes during his campaign in Greece (VII. 197). The anthropologist Alfred Adler, in a recent article on the rites of kingship in an African tribe, reiterates that there seems little doubt that cults of sacrificial kingship once existed widely.

Whether from ritual sacrifice or plain murder, Prince Meriadoc and Princess Orwen are rescued from a particularly horrible fate, and their foster parents carry them to safety from Arglud into the deep forest. The forest is called Fleventana in the Cotton manuscript and Eleventana or possibly Cleventana in the Rawlinson. The location is identified as the border between Arthur's kingdom and King Urien's Scotland because this is the point where the escort for King Urien under Sir Kay turns back. The description of the nests of eagles is reminiscent of the description of Loch Lomond by Geoffrey of Monmouth (ix. 6). If Arglud is Dumbarton, then Loch Lomond would not have been far away.

The four fugitives remain hidden in the forest, living in a cave, and subsisting on hunting and gathering. The description of

Introduction

steaming the meat using a pair of pits dug six inches apart, one for water to be heated by hot rocks or coals, connected by a steam vent to the second pit where the meat is covered in leaves, is a classical cooking technique. The Boy Scouts have used this system, saying there was a tradition that the Romans had invented it.

The *Enfances* of Meriadoc end with the separation of the brother and sister as each is carried off from this idyllic existence and thrust into adulthood, the princess as the captured bride of King Urien and the prince pressed into Arthur's army by Sir Kay.

The second group of analogues is centered on the "Combat at the Ford." The author portrays the combats between Meriadoc and the Black Knight, the Red Knight, and the White Knight as judicial battles. These are clearly court cases over ownership of forest land which are to be decided by the wager of battle, but instead of the duels taking place before the king and his council, the locations of these combats are at remote fords. Even though the author takes care to explain that these fords mark the boundaries of the properties in question, this does suggest that the folklore of the defense of a ford may be in the material that the author is using.

Bruce first proposes that the "Three-day Tournament" motif lies behind the encounters in *Meriadoc*, citing "Gareth," Chapters 7-10 (1913, p. xxxii), but these encounters in "Gareth" are not tournaments; the three-day tournament motif occurs at Chapters 26-30, where Gareth rides in a variety of colors. Although this material seems to be confused, Bruce's suggestion bears further consideration. The three-day tournament occurs in other versions of the "Fair Unknown" pattern. For example, Ipomydon rides to the tournament with three different horses and trappings: "That one was whyte as any mylke; the trappure of hym was whyte sylke;/ That other was rede, bothe styff and stoure,/ The trappure was of the same coloure;/ Blake than was that othir stede,/ of the same coloure was his wede" (Ikegami, ll. 645-650). The colors black, red, and white are features of some versions of the three-day

tournament, but in *Meriadoc* they are worn by the opponents, not by the hero.

Loomis, on the other hand, identifies the underlying motif as "The Combat at the Ford." A stock incident in many Arthurian romances, it occurs in *Erec, Diu Krône, Le Bel Inconnu,* Wauchier's *Continuation,* Malory's "Gareth," *Lanzelet, Lai de l'espine,* and *Eger and Grime,* as well as *De ortu Waluuanii* and *Meriadoc.* Loomis relates a number of these incidents, including the "Gareth," to each other with the details of a thorn bush by the ford and the opponents who wear distinctive single-colored armor: in the *Didot Perceval,* the opponent is Urbain, son of the Queen of the Blackthorn; in the *Lai de l'espine,* a red knight at the Ford of the Thorn; in *Diu Krône,* Gazosein, who wears a white shirt at the ford "Noirespine"; and in "Gareth," the Black Knyght of the Black Launde near a black hawthorn, but without a ford (1945–1946, pp. 63–71).

Mullen adds the encounter between Arawn and Havgan at the ford in *Pwyll*. Although no thorn tree is present, the distinctive clothing is: Arawn is dressed in grey and Havgan in "summer white" (p. 24). Loomis and Mullen agree that even though the encounters with the three knights in *Meriadoc* have no thorn bush mentioned, they are related to the Celtic myth that underlies these other encounters at the ford in the Arthurian legends.

Another distinctive feature of the duels at the fords in *Meriadoc* is that Arthur does not eat until he hears the result of the duel each day; and on the day that Meriadoc takes the challenge, he does not allow his men to eat either. Mullen notes variants of this motif in "Gareth," *Gawain and the Green Knight,* the first continuation of *Conte del Graal,* and the *Queste del Saint Graal* (p. 26). In *Meriadoc,* however, this delaying of the meal seems to be motivated by anxiety over the duel (Gowans, p. 86) and may even represent a ritual of fasting before a judicial duel.

After Meriadoc has defeated the Black Knight in the judicial duel, he returns to the court leading the defendant. Arthur, anxious over the outcome, has ordered a lookout on the walls to

see who is returning. The author then uses a motif known as the "watchman device" to add to the suspense of the moment (Sims-Williams, pp. 83–117). The watchman describes the gait of the horses, the armor first of Meriadoc and then the Black Knight, and finally the important detail—that it is Meriadoc who is leading the Black Knight. The "watchman device" in this section of *Meriadoc*, however, may not have a specific source in folklore, particularly with the watchman's description of Meriadoc's classical array: the coat of mail with triple links of gold, like the prize awarded Mnestheus in the *Aeneid*, Book 5, or the halter with the golden bit, like those of the horses given by Latinus to the Trojans, Book 7.

At the end of each duel in *Meriadoc*, the defeated knight swears fealty to Meriadoc, and Meriadoc is able to manipulate Arthur into restoring the property he has won from him in battle. Bruce suggests a number of analogues: *Erec, Vengeance Raguidel, The Awntyrs off Arthure* and *Golagros and Gawane* (1913, p. xxxii, n. 2). Of these the encounter of Gawain and Galerone in *The Awntyrs off Arthure* is the closest and I will discuss it in more detail later, considering the possibilty of influence.

The third group of episodes is centered on "The Faery Mistress." After the judicial duels are over, Meriadoc and his three new companions, the Black Knight, the Red Knight, and the White Knight, take service as mercenaries under the Emperor of the Alemanni. In pursuit of the Emperor's enemies, they inadvertently enter an enchanted forest. The author explains the nature of the forest and the subsequent otherworldly adventures:

> Huge fierce beasts inhabited it, and uncounted and unbelievable apparitions troubled and confused those who wanted to cross it. In fact every variety of phantasm became visible here in its outward appearance, so that not one of those crossing escaped unscathed by their deception. These phantoms, first by causing unreasoning fear, then by producing hallucinations, drove men one by

one out of their senses, snatched as if in a trance to another world (p. 115).

The author prepares the reader to watch Meriadoc and his contingent confused by a sun that rises and sets too quickly, astounded by a marble palace where none had stood before, and mystified by the beautiful lady who is its castellan. Analogues of the "Faery Mistress" show a wide range of examples of the Celtic fairy mistress and her castle. Mullen summarizes much of the material, emphasizing the plain where the castle is seen as a version of the Irish Mag Mell, "The Plain of Delight." The castle that appears where none was before is in Irish folklore, the Welsh *Manawydan, Son of Llyr,* as well as Chrétien's *Conte del Graal* (pp. xxxvi, 27–34). Bruce notes versions where the meal is eaten in silence in *Huon of Burdeux, Sir Degree, Les Mervelles de Rigomer,* and *Ogier le Danois* (1913, p. xxxiii), to which Mullen adds *Perlesvaus* and *Owain or the Lady of the Fountain*. Mullen concludes that "The lovely damsel is none other than the conventional Fairy Mistress who has contrived a meeting with her mortal lover and wishes him to remain with her in the Other World" (p. 34).

The author of *Meriadoc*, however, indicates that this particular Lady is not all she seems to be. In an irony he develops between what the reader knows and what Meriadoc must guess, he displays the iconography of Fortuna with the gaming scene. Significant also for Fortuna's role in kingship, which he had noted at the beginning of the romance, is the description of her abode at the top of the porphyry stairs. Even the rushing river that forms the boundary of the otherworld in this romance is sometimes part of the iconography of Fortuna.

Fortuna as the controlling goddess appears in other Arthurian romances, most notably in *Wigalois, The Knight of Fortune's Wheel* (composed ca. 1200–1215) where the young knight's destiny is sometimes personified as Dame Fortune. Wirnt

von Grafenberg treats this destiny within a Christian context, whereas the author of *Meriadoc* does not.

In the introduction to *Wigalois*, the translator J. W. Thomas proposes an intriguing possibility, saying that "It is likely that Wirnt's *diu saelde* is based on Renaud's fairy, who, toward the end of *Le Bel Inconnu* (ca. 1185–1190), tells the hero that it has been her power which has guided and led him throughout his adventures. The transformation she undergoes at Wirnt's hand is considerable and ingenious, but the role she plays is unchanged" (pp. 29–30). Thomas also notes that Ulrich von Zatzikhoven's *Lanzelet* (ca. 1194–1205) is about a young man blessed by Fortune, and *diu saelde* has a prominent role in determining his destiny (p. 38). Thomas's insight into the role of the fairy in the *Le Bel Inconnu* and the subsequent development of the role of Dame Fortune in *Wigalois* should be investigated further for the understanding of the role of the Goddess Fortuna as Faery Mistress in *Meriadoc*. Further, the relationship of these representations of Fortuna with the Celtic Goddess of Sovereignty may explain much about the "commonplace" Faery Mistress in Arthurian tradition.

Meriadoc's testing at the second castle belongs to analogues of "The Perilous Castle." Laurence Harf-Lancner notes the relationship of this episode to others he classifies as "Le géant et la fée" (pp. 347–375). Mullen links it to the testing story of the Irish tale *Bricriu's Feast*, which in turn shares features with the *Carl of Carlisle* and the episode of Kay and the spit which occurs in the first continuation of *Le Conte del Graal* and *Golagros and Gawane* (pp. 34–43). In *Meriadoc*, however, it is the hero, not Kay, who is shamed.

The motif of the apparently empty castle is common and links this adventure to a number of tales, including those of the Waste City and Yvain's *Pesme Aventure* (Luttrell, pp. 197–202; Bózoky, pp. 349–356).

But the churls that Meriadoc must deal with are given slightly more iconographic identification than usual for this motif. In the

kitchen he confronts a churl who is a huge, beardless, hairless man. The churl strikes him with the spit. Meriadoc struggles with him and throws him into a well. When Meriadoc finally gets the food to his men and they are eating, another huge man armed with a "semitrabs" (half of a great beam or rafter), attacks them. These two belong to the Arthurian tradition, as the attacks on Kay with the spit mentioned earlier indicate, or the attacks by a log-throwing giant in other versions. Even Yvain confronts a pair of demon brothers in his analogous adventure. But there are some indications in this episode that the author was using other material, or else that he was aware of the pagan folklore in the pattern.

A specific pair of gods who are brothers is suggested by the iconography of the presentation in *Meriadoc*. Georges Dumézil, in *From Myth to Fiction: The Saga of Hadingus*, relates the records and myths of the worship of twins or brothers in Greek and Germanic tradition, drawing on the Spartan *Dioscuri* (Castor and Pollux in Roman mythology) and relating them to the two *Haddinjar*. In Vandal sources, the brothers are named Raos and Raptos. Essential to the iconography of the first brother is the beardless, hairless representation of a man who is always effeminate and wears a woman's wig in ceremonies. In mythology, this brother often meets death by drowning. The name of the second brother, "Raptos," is translated as "beam" or "rafter" (pp. 106–127). Dumézil concludes that "the earliest representation of the Spartan *Dioscuri* [was] represented, or doubtless symbolized, by two parallel beams linked together by crosspieces" (p. 117). The huge man in *Meriadoc* did not throw at Meriadoc's men simply a "trabs," "a beam or log or rafter" but a *semitrabs*, "half of a rafter." Considering that the author uses the prefix "semi," the term may echo the "half a rafter" that would characterize one of the two brothers. Three other details seem part of this complex of iconography: 1. The hit with the fist that Meriadoc takes earlier, and the association with boxing attested for the *Dioscuri* in Plutarch. 2. Meriadoc drowns the beardless man, throwing him

into the well. 3. The brother gods were Vanes, whose cult was considered shameful. Considering the Germanic links to the folklore of the *Enfances* of *Meriadoc*, the Germanic echoes in the episode of the castle where "no one who enters returns without shame" should also be investigated further.

The final group of episodes belongs to the "The Abduction" motif. In *Meriadoc*, the hero's quest is the rescue of the Emperor's daughter, abducted by Gundebald, King of the Land From Which No One Returns. The hero succeeds with the help of the Emperor's daughter, who presents him with the special horse fated to be ridden by the man who will kill the King. Loomis explores this motif as related to "The Violent Death of Curoi," where Blathnat gives the fatal sword to Cuchulainn (1943, 164–165). Mullen, looking for analogues where the gift includes the fatal horse, cites episodes in Chrétien's *Chevalier de la Charrette* and Ulrich von Zatzikhoven's *Lanzelet*. The general pattern has been identified as Stith Thompson's International Folktale Type 302, "The Ogre's Heart in the Egg" (Utley, pp. 596–607).

The square shape of Gundebald's castle is noted by Bruce to be like the Grail Castle in *Sone de Nausay* (1913, p. xxxiv), while A. C. L. Brown examines it as part of the tradition of square castles for the "Castle of Maidens," as well as in Irish folklore (pp. 359–370). However, the castle of Gundebald is not so much square as cross-shaped, with a defending tower at each of the four roads allowing access across a bog of tar. No other defensive wall was necessary because the tar pit allowed no access whatever.

The abduction of the Emperor's daughter and the confrontation with Gundebald can also be read as a variation of the folklore of the Irish Sovereignty. The Emperor's daughter, although a prisoner, has a strangely ambiguous position. She was abducted by force, but Gundebald treats her like a daughter. She inquires daily concerning the Emperor's military efforts on her behalf, yet she is Gundebald's valued advisor. She is the ranking administrator of the city in the absence of the king and the prefect. She even describes herself as the "potestas," "the sovereignty."

Yet she risks it all to help Meriadoc slay Gundebald. This extraordinary young woman embodies much of the Celtic otherwordly figure of the Sovereignty, who bestows royal rule(Goetinck, pp. 129–134).

Meriadoc wins his bride, but loses her and must win her again. This structure for a "bride winning" pattern has been studied extensively, with parallels in *Yvain, King Horn,* and even the *Odyssey* (Beatie, 104–107).

Meriadoc is an integral part of the body of material that makes up the Matter of Britain. It is also clearly part of the greater inheritance of stories that have survived in our culture from antiquity. While earlier critics have identified its relationships with the *Havelock* tales and to the Arthurian motifs of the Combat at the Ford, the Faery Mistress, The Perilous Castle, and The Abduction, more research needs to be done on the analogs that treat of the sacral kingship, the Goddess Fortuna, the churls of the Castle of Shame, and the Emperor's Daughter as the Sovereignty.

One final source needs to be considered, one that may be from history rather than folklore: the source for the decisive battle between the King of Gaul and the Emperor of the Alemanni. The war between the King of the Gaul and the Emperor of the Alemanni is to be decided by a pitched battle between the two armies, and that pitched battle is on a designated day in a designated place in an enclosed field, like a wager of battle on a national scale. This, of course, is romance, not history. M. Ashdown, investigating "Single Combat in English and Scandinavian Romance" (p. 121), mentions pitched battles in "hazeled" fields (marked with stakes): the battle of Vinheith in the *Egilssaga* (thought by some scholars to be a romanticized Battle of Brunnanburh), *Hkr.Hakonssaga*, Chap. xxiv, *Hkr. Olaf Tryggus*, Chap. xviii, *Orkneyingasaga*, Chap. xi.

It is possible that a reader familiar with the tradition would not so much take the designated field as a literal description but as the iconography of a battle between two armies that is as decisive as if it were a judicial single combat. The battle in

Meriadoc between the King of Gaul and the Emperor of the Alemanni is that decisive.

The final battle suggests one more analogue, one from history. The battle between Clovis, King of the Franks, and the Alemanni took place about the year 506 A.D., within the time frame for King Arthur. The battle at Tolbiac (Zulpich) brought relief from the raids of the Alemanni on the frontier; the remnant of the Alemanni swore allegiance to Clovis. It was at this battle that Clovis embraced Christianity, and it was this battle that helped establish the territory of what eventually became the kingdom of France (Wallace-Hadrill, pp. 168-169).

The author of *Meriadoc* is known to have been familiar with Gregory of Tours' *Historia Francorum*. Bruce and others note that the names of Gundebald, Guntramn, and Moroveus probably were borrowed from Gregory. Gregory also is the primary authority for the battle of Clovis against the Alemanni. The author of *Meriadoc* apparently adapted the traditional material of his source to bring his hero out of Cambria and away from Arthur's realm so that he could be the victorious knight in a kingdom-shaping battle on the continent. It is probable that he had this specific historical battle as a model.

A study of analogues for Arthurian romance must consider not only possible sources but also possible influences. The first to consider is *The Awntyrs off Arthure at the Terne Wathelyne*, a late fourteenth-century poem that contains a judicial duel over property. The poem is in two divisions. The first tells about the appearance of the ghost of Guenevere's mother to Guenevere and Gawain. The second tells about the challenge of Sir Galeron, who asks for a judicial duel over the land he claims as his patrimony, land Arthur has bestowed on Gawain. Gawain takes up the challenge on his own behalf, and on the next day the proper legal procedure is followed. Both men are seriously wounded. Sir Galerone relinquishes his rights to Sir Gawain in admiration of his prowess. But Arthur, first bestowing new lands on Gawain, establishes Sir Galerone in the property for which he fought so

bravely. The decision over the property does not have the drama that the judicial duel in *Meriadoc* develops, but the fact that this is, first of all, a judicial duel over property, and second that Arthur does not let the outcome of the duel stand but administers his own decision in equity possibly echoes the episode in *Meriadoc*. One manuscript of *Meriadoc* was in England at this time; the second was copied close to this period.

The second romance that may show the influence of *Meriadoc* is Malory's "Tale of Sir Gareth." The similarity of the names of the Black Knyghte of the Black Launde and the Reed Knyghte of the Reed Launde to Niger Miles de Nigro Saltu and Roseus Miles de Roseo Saltu was noted by Bruce and Loomis. There are also a few details of style and incident that are shared by both romances.

Citing the *New English Dictionary*, Mullen points out that the Middle English "launde" and the Latin "saltus" are equivalent. He proposes that they derive from a common source (p. 21).

"Gareth" and *Meriadoc* share some broad similarity in plot, although the development in the two romances is quite different. Both Gareth and Meriadoc are protégés of Kay, but where Kay mocks Gareth, creating resentment, Meriadoc and Kay respect each other. Both Gareth and Meriadoc begin by requesting adventures far beyond their untested reputations, but Gareth makes his request as a boon from Arthur, and Meriadoc from Kay. Both men win the fealty of the knights that they defeat in single combat. Gareth is accompanied by Lynet, while Meriadoc's companions are the Black Knight, the Red Knight, and the White Knight. Gareth and Meriadoc both rescue their ladies and both are wed, but Gareth is prevented from consummating his love before marriage, while Meriadoc is not. Although the stories are somewhat alike, the differences are too profound to indicate a single shared source.

Yet as different as they are, it is surprising to find a few close stylistic details. First, both Meriadoc and Gareth are driven by terrible storms to take shelter in a castle that they would have preferred to have avoided. Meriadoc and his men have been

warned not to enter the castle "from which no one who enters returns without shame," and they attempt to wait out the storm. But the storm becomes so intense that they are forced to seek shelter. Gareth, too, is compelled by a storm to take shelter in the Castle of the Duke de la Rouse:

> "And thenne felle there a thonder and a rayne as heuen and erthe shold goo togyder... and ever it lyghtned and thondred as it had ben woode. At the last by fortune he came to a castel..." (Bk. VII.31, Spisak, p. 192, ll. 4-8).

The storm in Meriadoc is also beyond endurance:

> "Post meridiem aut[em] tempestas valida est eis exorta, scilicet vis venti cum inundacione pluvie et coruscacione fulminum terroribusque tonitruum..." "After noon a fierce storm came upon them, violent wind with sheets of rain, bolts of lightning, and terrifying claps of thunder" (pp. 131-132).

The use of the phrase "by fortune" by Malory possibly reflects the role of Fortuna that dominates the parallel episode in *Meriadoc*.

Interestingly, the apocalyptic simile "as heuen and erthe shold goo togyder" in Malory also appears in *Meriadoc* but in a different scene. When Meriadoc has defeated the Black Knight and spared his life, the Black Knight tells Meriadoc that "quam si celi et terre una adinvicem, me medio existente, fieret collisio." "The force of his blow is as if heaven and earth came together, with myself in between" (pp. 84-85).

The episode of Gareth at the Castle of the Duke de la Rouse (Bk. VII.32, Spisak, p. 192, ll.10-35) shares four additional motifs with *Meriadoc*, all from the later episode of Meriadoc at the fortified city of King Gundebald (pp. 162-169): 1. The dispute with

the porter. 2. The intervention of the Lady. 3. The Lady's hospitality. 4. The evil custom of single combat with the Lord.

1. The dispute with the porter:

"Meriadocus autem advocans ianitorem rogavit blande, ut sibi ianuas patefaceret...'Cuiates,' ait, 'estis? Pacificene an exploratores? ...Vos autem ite et vobis in suburbano hospicia capite.' "

"Thenne Syr Gareth rode vnto the barbycan of the castel and praid the porter fayr to lete hym into the castel. The porter ansuered vngoodely ageyne and saide, thow getest no lodgyng here."

"Cui Meriadocus: 'Ex Britonibus originem ducimus; regi Britannie diu militavimus.' "

" 'Fayr syr, say not soo, for I am a knighte of Kinge Arthurs. ...' "

2. The Lady watching from the tower in the absence of the lord of the castle:

"Dum hec ab illis geruntur, fortuitu filia imperatoris in turri muris contigua..."

"Thenne she yode vp into a toure ouer the gate..."

3. The Lady's hospitality.

"... sed post refeccioneme cene ...eum introduxit thalamis omnibusque refocillavit deliciis."

"Thenne was he sette unto souper and had many good dysshes... And shortly whan he had souped, his bedde was made there..."

4. In both romances, the encounter between the young knight and the lord of the castle, required by the lord's evil custom, is postponed until the lord returns, but here the parallel ends.

Whether Malory made use of *Meriadoc* itself, or some earlier version that the author of *Meriadoc* may have also known, or both, may never be completely decided, but the small details held in common suggest that he may have been familiar with the Latin text as well as manuscripts of the shared tradition in French.

Artistic Achievement

The primary achievement of the author of *Historia Meriadoci* lies in his narrative skills. He has taken the stuff of the Arthurian legend, possibly from a whole tale, as he implies, and developed it into a romance that has evil villains, fairy mistresses, suspense, humor, derring-do, plus theme and unity so that the result "makes sense." His prologue explains his purpose and method:

Because I consider Meriadoc's chivalrous exploits and distinguished career worthy of remembrance, I have decided to write his story. The record is embellished with tales of such prowess and such excellence that if I plodded through each episode one by one I should turn its sweetness into surfeit. Therefore, taking into account the benefit for my readers, I set out to confine it to a concise style, knowing that a pithy discourse that makes sense is worth more than a rambling tale empty of meaning (p. 3).

From these opening words, two points can be assumed. First, he worked from some record that was longer than his retelling. Second, he made an effort to condense and focus his material, bringing out the meaning that he perceived in it. In the previous section on the analogues, a broad picture of the material contained in the tale of adventure has been outlined. His artistic achievement is in the romance that he created from that material.

Of his accomplishments, the characterization of his villains is perhaps the best, and these villains set the plot in action. He has three superbly drawn evil rulers, Griffin, Gundebald, and the Emperor.

Griffin, brother to the good King Caradoc, is a splendid mix of good intentions, greed for power, and cold practicality. The author develops his character by his deeds and by the narrator's insight, but most significantly by describing the counsel that he listens to. Two scenes are particularly fine: first, the scene where the councilors manipulate first his concern for the kingdom and then his pride; and second, the scene with his councilors when the decision is made to slay his brother's children. In the first the councilors take control; in the second Griffin, now seasoned in villainy, needs no help in perceiving the necessity of murder.

The Emperor, on the other hand, decides to betray Meriadoc without taking counsel with any of his lords and advisors. Driven by weakness in resisting the inroads of the Gauls, he makes a dubious alliance with their King, using his daughter's hand to confirm it. Then in a rousing speech before his councilors, he reasons with them why her champion Meriadoc must be condemned to death—never admitting that he had secretly sanctioned their betrothal.

While Griffin is a capable man acting as a king but without the strength of the truly royal right, the Emperor has the royal right, but lacks the integrity to rule with justice. Both men and kingdoms face war as a result. Griffin is replaced by the hereditary claimant; the Emperor and his descendants lose their domain.

Introduction

Griffin begins the plot; the Emperor closes it. Between the two are King Arthur and King Gundebald – the ideal good king and the ultimately evil one. Yet the author adds some complexity to even these stock figures.

The author depicts the character of Arthur as the king with both royal right and capability to rule. But even Arthur is not perfect. His pride and his royal prerogative almost lead him to injustice, but in the end he listens to his councilors.

King Gundebald, King of the Land from which No One Returns, is the ultimate enemy. He has deliberately broken the peace with a crime beyond pardon. He has kidnapped the only daughter of the Emperor of the Alemanni and he will not accept ransome for her return.

His castle is described as being in the center of a bituminous pit. "Slime pit" is the term the King James Bible uses to describe such a geological formation in Gen. 14.10. Isaiah describes "streams of pitch" in the cursed land of Edom (34.9), and "They shall name it No Kingdom There" (Revised Standard, 34.12). If the pitch were burning it would turn the scene into the traditional Hell.

But Gundebald is not without a redeeming feature: he has treated his captive with honor – as a daughter and as his sovereign lady. She is his most respected counselor and advisor. She is the administrator of his city in the absence of the King and his prefect. But the King will not return the maiden to her father, and the lands of two kingdoms suffer devastation because of his lawlessness. The King must die so that justice and peace may be restored.

Young Meriadoc tries to cope with these four rulers in his own quest for justice. The quest begins with his simple, childish plea for mercy from his uncle. Whether his near death from hanging on the oak is intended to blacken Griffin's character beyond all mercy, or whether, like Woden, Meriadoc survives hanging to gain a new dimension of wisdom, he is marked by an obsession for justice. He pursues the revenge for his father's death through due process in Arthur's court. He manipulates Arthur into

giving justice to the Black Knight of the Black Forest and the other knights. When he leaves his own inherited realm to take service with the Emperor and to restore justice by rescuing his daughter from King Gundebald, he finds he must sacrifice the kingdom he has won in battle in order to abide by his word to the Emperor, a crisis of justice that he explains in a carefully reasoned speech to his councilors. But the author does not let Meriadoc or the reader rest with the triumph of justice yet. Meriadoc is betrayed by the Emperor he has supported. He learns to beware power politics overriding a great man's given word. In the world of the romance—and possibly the real world it mirrors—royal justice is not so much law as personal honor. The final line of the romance is a great tribute to Meriadoc: "Meriadocus vero in omni probitate consenuit" (Meriadoc, in truth, lived to the end of his days in all honor).

The suspense and humor are developed when Meriadoc's sense of justice and the power struggles of Griffin, Arthur, Gundebald and the Emperor come into direct conflict. The suspense of the threatened children dominates the first part, a suspense that begins for the reader as soon as the councilors begin to manipulate Griffin, and it is sustained until Arthur's council brings in a sentence of death for the usurper. In contrast, Arthur's role as a just king is established before the judicial duels concerning the forest land arise; all that is at stake is the royal pride. So Meriadoc's action in restoring the knights' property, a reversal of expectation, has rich humor. A reversal of expectation also shapes the action in the final episodes, but the stakes are life or death for the hero. Meriadoc (and the reader) have trusted the Emperor. The author has given no clues to the reader to be wary of this man. Only by a careful rereading of the text does the reader realize the author also gave no clues that this man could be trusted. The Emperor's betrayal of Meriadoc and his own daughter is coolly rational, and it is shocking. The personal vengeance of the last scene seems just.

Introduction

The sense of mystery that enriches the story comes from the Arthurian material. This is most clearly evident in the action that takes place in the Enchanted Forest. Meriadoc's entrance into the Otherworld operates on several levels. In one sense, it is comic relief for the reader in a serious tale of a quest for justice. The author takes the reader into his confidence, explains what is happening, and allows the reader the pleasure of understanding Meriadoc's predicaments while Meriadoc is struggling to figure it all out. In another sense, however, the entrance into the Otherworld is what it has always been in legend, an initiation for the hero. The mystery remains for Meriadoc. Meriadoc must investigate, act rationally, protect his men, and maintain his integrity, even though the rules and expectations of the "real" world no longer apply. He passes the tests. He accepts as fact that he no longer has the blessing of Fortuna, his "royal luck." He must depend instead on the classical virtue of courage, which he demonstrates dramatically at the fortress of armed men, where with his back to the wall he continues to defend himself. He wins the approval and the admiration of these Otherworldly warriors. Then he meets the Weeping Lady, the final Otherworldly figure who is probably Fortuna in another guise. She gives him one more test of courage and sees that he is remounted on a knight's charger. Soon after he finds his missing men "by the favor of Fortuna" and together they emerge from the Enchanted Forest.

The artistic achievement of *Meriadoc* lies in a story well told, full of action and suspense. The theme of royal justice gives it unity and meaning. The traditional Arthurian materials add a dimension of mystery and terror. Even though composed in Latin for a medieval audience, the story has the timeless appeal of an idealistic young man's successful confrontation with entrenched power.

Editorial Policy For This Text and Translation

Historia Meriadoci, Regis Cambrie is represented in two manuscripts, British Library Cotton Faustina B vi, ff. 1r–23r, and Bodleian Rawlinson B 149, pp. 91–132. The Cotton Faustina manuscript is the older, identified as early fourteenth century. The title, in a different hand, is given as "Vita Meriadoci Regis Cambriae." The name of Robertus Cotton Bruceus is on the top and bottom margins of the first folio (plate 1). Immediately following are two other works related to the Arthurian legend: *De ortu Waluuanii*, 23r to 38r, and "Britones a troianis duxerunt originem," 38r to 40v, an abridgment of Geoffrey of Monmouth's *Historia Regum Britannie*. All three works are in the same fourteenth-century hand, undamaged and apparently complete. Making up the rest of Cotton Faustina B vi, part. 1, are various historical materials: annals, lists of kings, roster of the monks of Croxden, papal letters, the obituary calendar of the Nunnery of Daunton in Kent, records of financial matters for Canterbury Cathedral. Part 2 is the Middle English poem *The Desert of Religion*.

The text contains two columns of 35 lines on each folio. The script is Gothic textura. The script style approximates that of the scribe of Jacobus de Voragine, *Legenda Sanctorum*, 1312, Paris, as illustrated by S. H. Thomson, *Latin Bookhands of the Later Middle Ages* (Cambridge, 1969). A wide range of abbreviations is used: single letters, shortened words, suprascript letters, and various symbols. Initial letters in red and blue are calligraphic. The intials are infilled with spirals and dots. Some of the flourishes descending in the lower margins are cut off by trimming. The capitals within the text are infilled with yellow. Beginning on folio 1v, line drawings appear at random in the margins. Most are profile caricatures. These predate the present binding. On folio 19v there is slightly more detailing on the sentence capitals, two with little faces. Faded spots in the text as reproduced on

Introduction xlvii

microfilm are actually wax drippings. Capitalization and punctuation in the manuscript are systematic. Three capitals indicate a new story, two capitals a chapter or paragraph, a single capital a sentence. The capitalization of proper names varies. The punctuation within the sentence separates main grammatical divisions, but it is not completely consistent. Quoted material may be bracketed in the margin or underlined.

The Rawlinson MS B 149, on the other hand, is a much simpler production (plate 2). The codex is smaller, a vellum octavo of 135 folios. It is bound in a single sheet of vellum, lettered in ink, possibly original with the contents. The cover is laced onto the folios with a thong. The scribal hand is variously dated from the later fourteenth century (Macray's catalog of the Rawlinson collection) and early fifteenth century (Madan, cited by Morriss, p. 599). On the inside of the cover is a table of contents in the hand of Gerard Langbaine and a note: "Suum cuique: Tho. Hearne, Dec. 29, 1772, at wch time I bought this MS." Another note at the end says: "Dec. 29, 1722 2gs 1/2. Mr. Cls -1."

The contents of B 149 from the Rawlinson catalog are as follows:

> 1. *Historia Trium Magorum, sive trium regum Coloniae* (p.1). 2. *Narratio de Arthuro Rege Britanniae et Rege Gorlagon lycanthropo* (p.55). 3. *De Tirio Appolonio narratio* (p. 65). 4. *Historia Meriadoci, regis Cambrie, cum prologo brevi cujusdam R.* (p. 91). 5. *Liber Alexandri Philippi Macedonum qui primus regnavit in Grecia et preliis ejusdem* (p. 133). 6. *Tractatus, Aristotelis dictis, de regimine sanitatis, libris decem.Cum prologis Philippi et Johannis filii Patricii* (p. 207).

The *Meriadoc* entry on the verso of the cover in Langbaine's hand is "4 R. *Historia Meriadoci Regis Cambriae*. 91." "R." is given in the position of the author's name.

The entire book, representing a collection of medieval Latin romance, is the work of a single scribe. The letters at the paragraph divisions are usually touched with red, but not consistently. The pages are numbered as pages, not as folios. There are twelve pages in a gathering, with a linking word in the bottom margin at the end of each gathering. The manuscript is not damaged, but pages lack corners, and the scribe adjusts his lines to fit these, indicating imperfections in the original material. Some pages are quite thin, allowing the ink to show through. This does not create a problem for reading the original, but does make a photocopy difficult to read.

Although Bruce stated about the manuscripts, "Obviously, moreover, neither is copied from the other" (1913, xxiv, note 2), the relationship of the two manuscripts is quite close. Working with both, I conclude that the Rawlinson is a transcription of the Cotton Faustina. There is almost no substantive difference between the two texts. The scribe of the Rawlinson corrects errors and changes some of the medieval orthography, adding or subtracting "h"; double letters, "bl" for "ll," "d" for "t" in final position, and so on. The most positive indication of direct copying is in the section where the author describes the elaborate technique for preparing meat without cooking vessels. Here the Cotton manuscript has the term *clusilla*, meaning "barrier" or in this context, a "valve" or merely the spike that shuts off the channel for the steam. The scribe of the Rawlinson saw this possibly unfamiliar word with the "c" and "l" ligatured and perceived the "d" of the curve and the long stroke. So the Rawlinson MS reads *dusilla*.

In preparing this edition, I have used Bruce's 1913 edition, microfilm, and the manuscripts themselves. I have attempted to present the text as it is contained in the Cotton Faustina, the older text, incorporating the corrections that the Rawlinson scribe made when necessary. I have reproduced the divisions of the manuscripts with large initial letters. I have followed the manuscript carefully in regard to sentence division for the edition,

Introduction

except in two or three places where the sentence in the manuscripts had no main verb. Bruce's edition, prepared from handwritten copy, contains some typographical errors and omissions which, along with variant readings from his edition, are noted in the apparatus. I have used "v" for consonantal "u." I have retained non-classical spelling for words which are medieval variants.

The translation is also conservative. While not quite a word-for-word translation, I have tried to present it sentence by sentence, dividing the sentences into smaller units only when the Latin sentence length becomes unwieldly. Paragraphing in the English follows modern conventions.

A project of this scope is rarely the work of one person alone. I want to thank many friends for their help: J. F. Verbruggen, first, for his help with military terms and tactics; Jean-Claude Lozac'hmeur, Linda Gowans, Neil Wright, Morfydd E. Owen, Duey J. White, Jean Jost, and John and Caitlín Matthews for sharing their research; Armel Diverres, Faith Lyons, and Dhira Mahoney for reading part of the work-in-progress; and Mary Flowers Braswell and Valerie Lagorio for their valuable suggestions. I am particularly grateful to editors Lowry Nelson, Jr., and James J. Wilhelm for working with me toward a final draft of the text and translation. My special thanks to my mother, Marjory Moore Leake, my first Latin teacher, who joined in this project with expertise and unfailing enthusiasm, and to my husband, Jim Houston Day, Sr., whose encouragement made it possible.

Select Bibliography

Editions

Bruce, James Douglas, ed. "*Vita Meriadoci*, an Arthurian Romance." *PMLA*, *13* (1900), 327–414.

———, ed. *Historia Meriadoci* and *De ortu Waluuanii*. Hesperia 2. Göttingen: Dandenhoed & Ruprecht, 1913.

Criticism and Study Guides

Adams, Henry. *Mont-Saint-Michel and Chartres*. New York: Houghton, 1933.

Arthur, Ross. "The *judicium Dei* in the *Yvain* of Chrétien de Troyes," *Romance Notes*, *28.1* (Fall, 1987), 3–12.

Ashdown, M. "The Single Combat in Certain Cycles of English and Scandinavian Tradition and Romance." *Modern Language Review*, *17.2* (1922), 113–130.

Bale, John. *Index Britanniae Scriptorum*. Ed. R. L. Poole and M. Bateson. London: Oxford, 1902.

———. *Scriptorum Illustrium Majoris Brytanniae ... Catalogus*. 2 vols. Basil: Oporium, 1557–1559; microcard, Louisville: Lost Cause Press, 1959.

Beatie, Bruce A. "Patterns of Myth in Medieval Narrative." *Symposium*, *25* (1971), 101–122.

Bozóky, Edina. "Roman médiéval et conte populaire: le château désert." *Ethnologie française*, *4* (1974), 349-356.

Brown, Arthur C. L. *The Origin of the Grail Legend.* Cambridge, Mass.: Harvard University Press, 1943.

Bruce, James Douglas. *The Evolution of Arthurian Romance from the Beginning Down to the Year 1300.* 2 vols. Baltimore: 1928; rpt. Gloucester, Mass.: Peter Smith, 1958.

Brugger, Ernst. "Zu *Historia Meriadoci* und *De Ortu Walwanii.*" *Zeitschrift für französische Sprache und Literatur,* 46 (1923), 247–280, 406–440.

Day, Mildred Leake, ed. and trans. *The Rise of Gawain, Nephew of Arthur (De Ortu Waluuanii Nepotis Arturi).* Garland Library of Medieval Literature, Volume 15, Series A. New York: Garland Publishing Inc., 1984.

Deutschbein, Max. *Studien zur Sagengeschichte Englands.* Cöthen: 1906.

Dumézil, Georges. *From Myth to Fiction: The Saga of Hadingus.* Chicago: University of Chicago Press, 1973.

Foerster, Wendelin, ed. *Li Chevaliers as deus espées: Altfranzösisches Abenteuerroman.* Halle: Max Niemeyer, 1877; rpt. Amsterdam: Rodopi, 1966.

Ford, Patrick K., trans. *The Mabinogi and Other Medieval Welsh Tales.* Berkeley: University of California Press, 1977.

Frazer, Sir James George. *The New Golden Bough.* Ed. Theodor H. Gaster. New York: Phillips, 1959.

Galyon, Aubrey. "*De ortu Walwanii* and the Theory of Illumination." *Neophilologus,* 62 (1978), 335–341.

Gates, Robert J., ed. *The Awntyrs off Arthure at the Terne Wathelyne.* Philadelphia: University of Pennsylvania, 1969.

Geoffrey of Monmouth. *Historia Regum Britanniae.* Ed. Acton Griscom. London: Longmans, 1929.

Goetinck, Glenys. *Peredur: A Study of Welsh Tradition in the Grail Legends.* Cardiff: University of Wales, 1975.

Gout, Paul Émile. *Le Mont-Saint-Michel: Histoire de l'Abbaye et de la Ville.* 2 vols. Paris: Libraire Armand Colin, 1910.

Gowans, Linda. *Cei and the Arthurian Legend.* Woodbridge, Suffolk: D. S. Brewer, 1988.

Graves, Robert. *The Greek Myths.* 2 vols. Rev. ed. Harmondsworth, Middlesex: Penguin, 1960.

———. *The White Goddess.* New York: Farrar, Straus, Giroux, 1948.

Harf-Lancner, Laurence. *Les Fées au Moyen Âge.* Geneva: Slatkine, 1984.

Henry of Huntington. "Letter to Warinus." In Léopold Delisle, ed., *Chronique de Robert de Torigni.* Rouen: Société de l'Histoire de Normandie, 1872–1873. I: 97–119.

Herodotus, ed. and trans. A. D. Godley. New York: Putman's, 1921.

Hilka, Alfons. *Vollmölers Kritischer Jahresbericht über die Fortschritte der romanischen Philologie,* 9.11 (1911), 82–83.

Ikegami, Tadahiro, ed. *The Lyfe of Ipomydon.* Seijo English Monographs, 21. Tokyo: Seijo University, 1983.

Lea, Henry Charles. *The Duel and the Oath.* 1866, rpt. Philadelphia: University of Pennylvania Press, 1974.

Loomis, Roger Sherman. *Celtic Myth and Arthurian Romance.* New York: Columbia University Press, 1927.

———. "The Combat at the Ford in the Didot *Perceval*," *Modern Philology, 43* (1945–1946), 63–71.

———. "The Latin Romances." In *Arthurian Literature in the Middle Ages.* Oxford: Clarendon, 1959. Pp. 472–479.

———. "More Celtic Elements in 'Gawain and the Green Knight.'" *Journal of English and German Philology, 42* (1943), 149–184; rpt. *Studies in Medieval Literature: A Memorial Collection of Essays by R. S. Loomis.* Ed. Dorothy Bethurum Loomis. New York: Burt Franklin, 1970. Pp. 157–192.

Lozac'hmeur, Jean-Claude. "Recherches sur les origines indo-européennes et ésotériques de la légende du Graal," *Cahiers de civilisation médiévale, 30* (1987), 45–63.

Luttrell, Claude. *The Creation of the First Arthurian Romance.* Evanston, Ill.: Northwestern University Press, 1974.

Morriss, Margaret Shove. "The Authorship of the *De ortu Waluuanii* and the *Historia Meriadoci.*" *PMLA, 23* (1908), 599–608.

Mullen, William B. "A Critical Study of the *Historia Meriadoci.*" Diss. Columbia, 1951.

Olson, Oscar Ludvig. *The Relation of the Hrolfs Saga Kraka and the Bjarkarimur to Beowulf.* Chicago: The University of Chicago, 1916.

Patch, Howard Rollin. *The Goddess Fortuna in Medieval Literature.* Cambridge, Mass.: Harvard University Press, 1927.

Rajna, Pio. "Per le origini e la storia primitiva del Ciclo brettone." *Studii Medievali*, 3 (1930), 201–257.

_____. "Sono il *De ortu Waluuanii* e l'*Historia Meriadoci* Opera de un Medesimo Autore?" *Medieval Studies in Memory of Gertrude Schoepperle Loomis*. Ed. R. S. Loomis. Paris: Champion, 1927. 1–20.

Rank, Otto. *The Myth of the Birth of the Hero*. Ed. Philip Freund. Nervous and Mental Diseases Monographs. New York, 1959.

Robert of Torigni. *The Chronicle of Robert of Torigni, Abbot of the Monastery of St. Michael-in-Peril-of-the-sea*. Ed. Richard Howlett. *Chronicles of the Reigns of Stephen, Henry II, and Richard I*. Vol. 4. London: Master of the Rolls of Great Britain, 1889.

_____. *Chronique de Robert de Torigni Abbé du Mont-Saint-Michel Suivré de Divers Opuscules Historiques...* Ed. Léopold Delisle. 2 vols. Rouen. Libraire de la Société de l'Histoire de Normandie, 1872–1873.

Sims–Williams, Patrick. "Riddling Treatment of the 'Watchman Device' in *Branwen* and *Togail Bruidne da Derga*," *Studia Celtica*, 12/13 (1977–1978), 83–117.

Smail, R. C. *Crusading Warfare (1097–1193)*. Cambridge: Cambridge University Press, 1956.

Spisak, James W., ed. *Caxton's Malory*. 2 vols. Berkeley: University of California Press, 1983.

Thomas, J. W., trans. Wirnt von Grafenberg. *Wigalois, The Knight of Fortune's Wheel*. Lincoln: University of Nebraska Press, 1977.

Utley, Francis Lee. "Arthurian Romance and International Folktale Method." *Romance Philology,* 17 (1964), 596–607.

Van de Vyer, A. "L'Unique victoire contre les Alamans et la conversion de Clovis en 506," *Revue belge de philologie et d'histoire,* 15 (1938), 793–815.

Verbruggen, J. F. *The Art of Warfare in Western Europe during the Middle Ages from the Eighth Century to 1340.* Trans. Sumner Willard and S. C. M. Southern. Amsterdam: North-Holland, 1977.

Wallace-Hadrill, J. M. *The Long-Haired Kings.* 1962; rpt. Toronto: University of Toronto Press, 1982.

Warren, W. L. *Henry II.* Berkeley: University of California Press, 1973.

Wieber, James Leon, trans. "A Translation and Literary Study of *De ortu Walwanii,* a Thirteenth-Century Romance." Diss. Michigan State University, 1974.

Zenker, R. *Zur Mabinogionfrage.* Halle, 1912.

The Story of Meriadoc, King of Cambria

Historia Meriadoci, Regis Cambrie

Historia Meriadoci, Regis Cambrie

Incipit prologus R. in Historia Meriadoci, regis Kambrie.

Memoratu dignam dignum duxi exarare historiam, cuius textus tantarum probitatum tantique leporis decoratur titulis, ut, si singula seriatim percurrerem, favi dulcorem in fastidium verterem. Legencium[1] igitur consulens utilitati illam compendioso perstringere stilo statui, sciens quod maioris sit precii brevis cum sensu oracio quam multiflua racione vanans locucio.[2]

Incipit Historia Meriadoci, regis Kambrie.

Igitur ante tempora regis Arturi, qui totius Britannie monarchiam obtinuit[3], insula tres in partes digesta, Kambriam videlicet Albaniam[4] et Loegriam, plurimorum regum subiacebat imperiis, eiusque quam plures, prout Fortuna rem ministrabat, uno in temporegubernacula sorciebantur. Ea autem tempestate regnante, scilicet, Uther Pendragon, patre

1 R. legentium
2 R. loqucio
3 F. optinuit
4 R. Cornubian.

The Story of Meriadoc

The prologue by R. introduces the History of Meriadoc, King of Cambria:

Because I consider Meriadoc's chivalrous deeds and distinguished career worthy of remembrance, I have decided to write his story. The record is embellished with tales of such prowess and such excellence that if I plodded through each episode one by one I should turn its sweetness into surfeit. Therefore, taking into account the benefit of my readers, I set out to confine it to a concise style, knowing that a pithy discourse that makes sense is worth more than a rambling tale empty of meaning.

The story begins:

It so happened that before the time of King Arthur, who secured the monarchy of all Britain, the island was divided into three parts: Cambria, Albany, and Logres. It was governed by many kings; and, since at that time the goddess Fortuna controlled human affairs, the reigns of these men were selected by lot. So it was that during the reign of Uther Pendragon,

Arturi, regnum Kambrie duobus germanis, genitore defuncto, cesserat quorum natu maior, Caradocus dictus, ius regium possidebat; iunior autem, Griffinus vocabulo, partem provinicie sibi a fratre gubernabat creditam. Sedes vero regni Caradoci regis et quo maxime (F. col. 2)[1] frequentare solebat penes nivalem montem, Kambrice Snavdone resonat, exstabat. Hic autem rex Caradocus, diviciis pollens miraque virtute preditus, classem per maximam milite instructam in Hyberniam duxit, quam, rege ipsius devicto, sue dicioni subiugans sibi tributariam effecit. Rebusque prospere gestis, filiam regis Hybernensis suo matrimonio copulavit, ex qua in Kambriam reversus, duos gemellos sed diversi sexus progenuit. Qui, dum regnum non modico tempore rexisset tranquille, contigit eum in senium vergi etateque prematura gravari. Et quia in effeto corpore et vigor minuitur et sensualis intellectus hebatatur, tanto regimini operam ulterius adhibere[2] non prevalens, tocius regni tutelam suo fratri Griffino tuendam tradidit. Ipse autem venatibus aliisque oblectamentis licencius indulgens quiete et ocio senium protrahebat et fovebat.

---

[1] F. et quo maxime *repeated*.
[2] F. adibire.

father of Arthur, the kingdom of Cambria passed to two brothers at the death of their father. The elder, Caradoc by name, held the full authority of the kingship; the younger man, Griffin, governed part of the realm as a trust to him from his brother. The capital city of King Caradoc and the place where he was most often in residence was under the snowcapped mountain the Cambrians called Snowdon.

This King Caradoc, possessing great wealth and commanding a splendid army, invaded Ireland with an enormous fleet. After the King of Ireland was slain, Caradoc subdued the country to his authority, requiring the Irish to pay him tribute. When the campaign was successfully completed, he took the daughter of the King of Ireland in marriage, and after they returned to Cambria, she bore him twin children, a son and a daughter. After Caradoc had ruled the kingdom for a considerable period of peace, it so happened that he began to age and to be afflicted with a premature senility. The vigor of his exhausted body diminished, and his perceptive mind became sluggish. As a consequence of being unable to direct the governing of the kingdom any longer, he transferred to his brother Griffin the maintenance of the defenses of the country. Caradoc eased and delayed the aging process with quiet and leisurely living, permitting himself to enjoy hunting and other pleasures whenever he wished.

At Griffinus curam regni sibi commissam diligenter exequens sapienterque administrans nilabsque regis Caradoci fratris sui consilio disponebat. Unde et a fratre maiorem graciam meruit, eique omnem regni potestatem, regio dumtaxat sibi retento nomine, rex Caradocus commiserit. Sed ubique nequicie pestis sur(F. f. 2v)repit, que eo cicius mentem ad scelus impellit, quo eam maior rerum cupido infecerit. Quidam namque perverse mentis, vel fraterne paci invidentes aut novitatibus stu(R. p. 92)dentes seu certe aliorum discrimen sibi lucrum fore reputantes, Griffinum conveniunt eumque in fraternam necem hiis verbis accendunt:

Quia tuis," inquiunt, "hactenus utilitatibus accuracius studium dedimus teque honoris sublimare fastigio sedulum habuimus, indignum nos valde ducere noveris, hunc decrepitum tibi preponi[1], quem omnium sensuum iam pene constat officio privari. Maximo quippe dedecori tibi debet videri, illi te dignitate posteriorem haberi, qui et eiusdem nobilitatis insigniris linea et cui maior cum virtute corporis noscitur inesse sapiencia. Iam eciam fama vulgante, comperimus illum ad sue nate coniugium quendam gentis extranee potentem accivisse regnique gubernacula tibi commissa ei velle

1   R. proponi

Yet Griffin, conscientiously accepting the responsibility for the defense of the kingdom that had been committed to him and administering it with wisdom, made no decisions of state without consulting his brother King Caradoc. So it was that he earned the sincere gratitude of his brother, and Caradoc entrusted to him all the sovereignty of the kingdom, retaining for himself the monarchy in name only.

But it was not long before a contagion of evil arose from many sources that infected Griffin's mind with villainy, so that he became obsessed with the desire for full kingship. For indeed certain persons of twisted mind — whether resentful of the peace of his brother or desiring greater power — or else certain others considering the potential wealth for themselves approached Griffin and incited him with these words to put his brother to death:

They said, "Because until now we have given very careful attention to your advancement, and we have seen you elevated in honor to the highest rank, you should be aware that the decrepit old man set above you is certainly unworthy to lead us — a man whom by now everyone knows is deprived of almost every use of his wits. It ought to be seen as the greatest shame for you to be beneath him in dignity: you have the same noble lineage and, in addition, superior power of body and intellect. Already the word is out that

committere. Quem si contigerit sibi oblata inisse[1] connubia, ratum existimes quod et te debito honore destituet et nobis avita predia prorsus[2] surripiet. Fraude quippe et subdolositate fieri ne dubites, te regiis prelatum negociis, donec prefatum nobilem filie intervenientibus (col. 2) nupciis sibi confederaverit; cuius amminiculo si quid adversus eum molire volueris, tuos casset conatus. Cur igitur illum infatuatum senem diucius sinis vivere, cuius causa et nos et tocius regni statum patet periclitar[i]?[3]. Verum tua tibi mens fortassis applaudit, omne ius regium ac omne semper sicut nunc tibi[4] regni cessurum negocium. Sed numquid impune? Nonne Caradoco educatur filius quem eciam nunc[5] etas tenella mire probitatis futurum certis manifestat indiciis? Nonne, cum viriles annos attigerit, sibi paternum vendicabit principatum? Cuius apicem si te consentaneo assequi non potuerit, numquid tibi invito vi extorquere non laborabit? Hinc civilis discordia, intestinum bellum, cedes civium, patrieque proveniet desolacio. Iube igitur ad Tartara dirigi cuius vitam nobis tanto perpendimus imminere discrimini. Ecce universa manus procerum tibi subditur, omnis regni potestas tue voluntati exponitur, si id dumtaxat perfeceris, quod tibi a nobis consulitur. Et ne causeris te tantum

1   F. in esse.
2   F. prossus.
3   R. &. F. periclitare.
4   R. tibi *added between lines*.
5   R. eas *marked for deletion*.

he has invited a certain powerful man from a foreign nation with regard to the marriage of his daughter, and he wishes to entrust to this man the authority of the kingdom committed to you. If this marriage treaty is successful, you may be assured both that he will strip you of your deserved honor and that he will certainly confiscate our ancestral estates. Do not doubt that by deception and cunning you will be passed over in the administration of the kingdom when the king has allied himself to that nobleman by the marriage of his daughter, and should you wish to oppose this man, the king, with this man's assistance, will crush your efforts. For this reason it is obvious that both we and the whole kingdom are in serious jeopardy. Why therefore do you allow this foolish old man to remain alive? Indeed possibly your own dreams have suggested that the full authority of the kingdom should be yours, and thus all royal power for all time. But surely not without a struggle? Is not Caradoc raising a son who even at his tender age is showing remarkable prowess? Will he not, upon reaching manhood, lay claim for himself the realm of his father? If he cannot gain the crown with your consent, will he not certainly fight to take it by force? Thus there will be civil discord, revolution, slaughter of innocent people, and desolation of the land. Order us therefore to deliver to Tartarus the man whose life we deem of such imminent danger to us. You are aware that the entire force of the nobility is obedient to you; the military strength of the whole

negocium absque magna industria manuque valida nec posse nec audere aggredi, tuum assensum tribue, et nos eo rem moliemur ingenio, quo nulla tibi de eius nece possit oriri suspicio. Quid multa? Hiis atque aliis multis fraudulentis ser(F. f. 3r)monibus animum Griffini circumveniunt et, nunc quasi imminente terrentes[1] discrimine, nunc blanda regni mulcentes ambicione, ad frat(R. p. 93)erne necis assensum pertrahunt. Inde loci temporisque opportunitas queritur, qua propositum perpetraretur facinus. Placet eum silvas venaturum adeuntem a sociis seducere et in abdita nemoris iaculo confodere.[2] Diesque crastina ad hec explenda statuitur, qua regem Caradocum venandi gracia silvas se aditurum proposuisse non ignorabant.

Nocte vero preterita ipsius diei, cum rex Caradocus se quieti dedisset, visum est sibi suum fratrem Griffinum sibi [in] silvis ex adverso consistere et duas sagittas pharetra exemptas cote diligenter acuere. Duosque deinde viros advenisse ipsasque sagittas de manu Griffini accipientes tenso nervo inopinate in se

---

1 R. trentes
2 F. confodire.

kingdom is at your disposal if you would only choose to carry out this action which we advise you. And lest you give as a reason that you yourself are neither capable nor daring enough to undertake such a task without great effort, support, and influence, grant your approval and we will undertake this plot with such cunning that no suspicion can arise against you concerning the death of this man."

What more? With these and many other cajoling words the mind of Griffin was beset, and these men — now alarming him with the crisis as if it were imminent, now soothing him with flattering dreams of the kingdom — drew from him his assent to the murder of his brother. At once they began to plan the time and place where the villainous deed could be done. It was decided to lead him away from his companions when he went into the forest to hunt and in a hidden grove stab him with a spear. The very next day was chosen to carry out the plan, for they were well aware that King Caradoc had made plans to go into the forest in the morning to hunt.

Indeed on the night before that day, when King Caradoc had gone to sleep, a dream came to him that his brother Griffin was lying in wait for him in the forest, carefully sharpening on a whetstone two arrows drawn from a quiver. And then two men came and received those arrows from the hand of Griffin and,

direxisse. Ad quarum ictum ipse perter[r]itus sompno excutitur, et, quasi revera vulnus pertullisset, magnis vocibus vociferatur. Cuius insolito clamore regina obstupefacta eum inter brachia corripit et quid haberet curve tantas voces emitteret tremebunda inquirit. Quo, adhuc pre timore palma pectori impressa, qui viderat referente, illa presaga futuri: "Te, domine," ait, "queso, observa, quia tuus procul dubio germanus Griffinus (F. f. 3r, col. 2) tibi machinatur insidias. Insidias quippe portendunt sagitte. Et quia te luce sequenti venatum ire constituisti, insidiarum locum tibi [in] silvis agnoscas parari. Laudo igitur te hac vice domi manere venatusque oblectamenta in posterum differre." E contra rex, "Desine," inquit, "loqui huiusmodi; meum fratrem quem adeo semper hactenus dilexi et cui tanta impertitus[1] sum beneficia mihi nunquam credam mortis velle moliri discrimina."

Consilio[2] itaque[3] regine cedere renuit, sed summo diluculo, ut fata eum ducebant, silvas venatum peciit. Griffinus autem, suus germanus, duos viros nobiles, quidem robustos et audaces sed moribus perversos, truculentos et sanguinis effusione gaudentes,

1 F. imperitu.
2 F. consio *corrected above the line*.
3 R. igitur.

drawing their bows, without warning they aimed at him and shot. Caradoc, terrified at the blow, was startled from sleep, and he screamed out as if he had actually been wounded. The queen, scarcely awake, threw her arms about him at this strange outburst and, shaking him, bent over him and asked why he had cried out so. To her, palms pressed to his chest from fear, he repeated what he had seen, and she, foretelling what would happen, said, "Lord, I beg you to watch out because without a doubt your brother Griffin is plotting against you. Arrows portend treachery. And because you have decided to go hunting at dawn, you must know the place of ambush is being laid for you in the forest. I urge you because of this to stay home and put off the enjoyment of the hunt until another day." Against this advice the king replied, "Stop talking like this. I could never believe that my brother, whom I have always loved so much and given such great benefits, would ever wish to conspire against my life."

He refused the advice of the queen; instead at first light, as the Fates led him, he set off for the forest to hunt. His brother Griffin had chosen two nobles who were strong and daring but also evil, cruel, and bloodthirsty; and he ordered them to carry out the

elegerat, destinatumque flagicium eis perficiendum commiserat, se eos omnibus Kambrie commorantibus sublimiores[1] facturum pollicitus. Regalis igitur familia dum discopulatis canibus inventam predam insequitur et, ut in tali solet fieri negocio, diversis viis certatim tenditur, rex Caradocus senio gravante insequi non prevalens solus cui mors imminebat deseritur. Nec mora, advolantes duo predicti scelesti viri non eminus inter densa fruticum[2] abditi[3] eum a via remocius in opaco recessu nemorum distrahunt, distractum iaculo confodiunt, ac, telo vulneri relicto, festinanter discedunt, ut pocius casu alicuius venantis (F. f. 3v) quam fraude insidiantis id evenisse creditur.

Mors autem[4] tanti viri diucius celari non potuit. Statim namque, adhuc tepente sanguine, a venatoribus silvas oberrantibus exanimis reperitur.[5] Fit clamor, turbo, tumultus, signoque dato, revo(R. p. 94)cantur caterve venancium. Profertur in medium funus regium cruore crudeliter conspersum, cuius miserabile spectaculum universos ad fletum commovet et planctum. Tam magni facinoris queruntur auctores, se difficile patet cognicio cuius rei de nullo habetur

1 F. sullimiores.
2 F. fructicum.
3 R. additi.
4 R. *repeated* autem.
5 F. repperitur.

wicked outrage, having promised them that he would make them the highest lords of Cambria. While the hunting party of the royal household was in pursuit of the quarry with the dogs running ahead, in their eagerness (as usually happens on a hunt) they all became separated. King Caradoc, not being able to keep up because of his infirmity, was left behind alone. For him death was imminent. Rushing forward immediately from their hiding place not far away in the tangled underbrush, the two assassins dragged him along the path even further into a remote, shadowy grove and, when they had him alone, ran him through with a hunting spear. They left quickly, leaving the spear in his body so that the death would seem to have been caused by an accident of someone hunting rather than by a deliberate plot.

The death of so great a man could not be concealed very long. Almost immediately his body was found by hunters ranging through the forest, the blood still warm. A shout was made, a commotion, an uproar; and with the blast of the horn, the parties of hunters were called back. The body, cruelly spattered with blood, was carried into the midst of the palace. The pitiful spectacle moved everyone to tears and breastbeating. The perpetrators of this great crime were sought but the facts were difficult to uncover

suspicio. Diffunditur rumor per vicinas urbes, regem Caradocum [in] silva insidiis circumventum crudeliterque peremptum. Omnes gemunt, omnes super eo[1] continuant luctum et gemitum, lacrimeque pro mortuo effuse quanto vivus habebatur testabantur amore.

Regina vero, dum hec geruntur, super visione sibi a viro relata nimis vera coniciens thalamo residebat seque inpacabili fletu afficiebat. Que, nece regis comperta eiusque funere eminus contemplato, inmodico dolore correpta in extasim corruit, et, quia mens respiracionem a dolore habere no potuit, corruens expiravit.

Interea vero Griffinus alias longius profectus[2] regia exequebatur negocia, ut omnis a se fratricidii aboleretur suspicio. Cui cum regis interfeccio nunciata (F. f.3v, col. 2) fuisset, scissa veste, abruptisque capillis, luctum simulavit, lacrimas ubertim effudit, set ipsas lacrimas pocius gaudium quam dolor extorquebat.

1   R. eum.
2   F. *marginal correction illegible.*

since there was no suspicion of anyone. The word spread through neighboring cities that King Caradoc had been ambushed in the forest and cruelly slain. All grieved, all remained in sorrow and mourning for him, and with streaming tears they offered a testimony of how much love was felt for this man when he was alive.

While all this was taking place, the queen, knowing too well the truth because of the dream told her by her husband, remained in her quarters, torturing herself with uncontrollable weeping. They told her of the king's death, and she watched the funeral from afar. Then, seized by overpowering grief, she fainted, and since her mind was unable to continue breathing because of her sorrow, she collapsed and died.

In the meantime, Griffin, who had traveled a long distance away, was carrying on the administration of the kingdom so that any suspicion of fratricide might be removed from him. When the death of the king was announced to him, he feigned grief by tearing his clothing and pulling out his hair; he shed tears copiously, but it was joy rather than pain that brought forth the tears.

Rege igitur Caradoco fatis dato ingentique omnium comprovincialium merore eius celebratis exequiis, Griffinus confestim vi et potencia regnum sibi arripuit, ipsiusque sibi iura vendicans, se, proceribus absentibus et nescientibus, diademate insignivit. Verum multociens nequiciam, quo magis quis tegere nititur, tocius[1] propalatur. Duo namque illi grassatores qui innocuum regis sanguinem effuderant[2] ie[3] semper assistentes, dum premium facinoris sibi promissum eum dissimulare et quasi oblivioni tradidisse[4] conspicerent, eum secrete convenere et ut debita prosolueret expeciere, se bene ab eo ea promeruisse commemorantes, quorum obsequio sibi regale cessisset solium. Ipse autem versipellis, locum se reperisse[5] advertens quo plebis a se opinionem averteret—de fratris namque interitu iam habebatur suspectus—totum facinus, quasi ultor fratris et rei in[s]cius, in eos retorsit et de morte sui germani coram regni magnatibus criminari cepit. Statimque quosdam ex officialibus advocans, "Hos," exclamat, "carnifices, hos

---

1 R. eo citius.
2 F. effuderunt.
3 R. ei *omitted*.
4 R. tradere.
5 F. repperisse.

When King Caradoc had been given over to his destiny and his funeral celebrated with deep mourning by all the people, Griffin immediately seized the kingdom by force and power and, claiming the legal rights to it in the absence of the nobility and without their knowledge, crowned himself.

But it is often true that the more someone strives to conceal villainy, the more completely it is revealed. The two assassins who had shed the innocent blood of the king remained in constant attendance on Griffin, and they soon came to the realization that not only was he failing to honor them as he had promised in payment for the crime, but also that he had consigned them, as it were, to oblivion. They went to Griffin privately and demanded that he pay what he owed, the reward deserved by those through whose obedience the royal throne had come to him. Since he was already being considered a suspect in his brother's death and wanted to avert the suspicion of the people from himself, that sly man, shifting from the original position he had devised, turned on the two as if he were his brother's avenger and knew nothing of the plot. He openly accused these important men of having committed the crime of the murder of his brother the king. Immediately summoning certain of the palace officials, he shouted, "These men are the

mei fratris karrissimi[1] interfectores tollite et eminencioris arboris fastigio tocius Kambrie simul suspendite, pateatque universis quibus eorum nequiciam remuneravi stipendiis!" Ad hec illi callide in eum (F. F.4r) cavillantes, "Nequiter," respondent, "exsolvis que nobis spopondisti." Quo sermone Griffinus perculsus metuensque ne se sceleris propalarent conscium eorum absque mora linguas radicitus iubet abscidi, ac, data sentencia, eos deinde puniri. Linguis (R. p.96) igitur precisis, ad supplicium pertrahuntur, ac in prospectu utriusque insule, Hybernie scilicet et Kambrie, rupe preruptissima una suspenduntur. Sermo tamen quem in Griffinum puniendi protulerant non surda aure perceptus ad principum patrie pervenit noticiam, unde apud omnes fratricidii Griffinus suspicionis notam incurrit.

Hoc itaque rumore vulgato, fit clandestina principum perpetratum facinus abhorrencium[2] convencio diligensque super rebus agendis inter eos consultacio. Nulli quippe dubium erat, sed, tum ex illorum qui crimen perpetrarant improbacione,[3] tum ex visionis

---

1   R. fratris mei carrissimi.
2   R. abhorrencium perpetratum facinus.
3   R. propetrarant improbatione.

murderers. Seize these killers of my beloved brother and hang them together from the highest tree of all Cambria, and let all the people know they have received payment for their crime!" To this those men railed at him hotly, "How shamefully you fulfill your oath to us!"

At these words Griffin was overcome with dread, and lest they reveal his complicity in their crime, without delay he ordered their tongues cut out and, as soon as the sentence was pronounced, for them to be executed. Tongueless, they were dragged to execution, and with the people of both lands, Ireland and Cambria, as witnesses, they were hanged together at a very steep rock. The words which the men about to be punished had uttered against Griffin came to the attention of the lords of the country and were understood by those who had ears to hear, so that among all men Griffin incurred the mark of suspected fratricide.

Since this rumor had become common knowledge, a secret meeting of the lords was called concerning the dreadful crime that had been committed; and a thorough consultation was made among them about the action they should take. None of them were in doubt—not only from the accusation by those men who had perpetrated the crime but also from the interpretation of the dream which we have

quam supra retulimus[1] interpretacione, omnes ratum habebant, regem Caradocum consensu et consilio Griffini, fratris sui, necatum fuisse. Callebantque viri sagacis ingenii, quod, si regni stabilimentum manusque validior Griffino provenisset, eamdem nequiciam quam in fratre exercuerat in se quoque qui ipsius fideles exstabant vel maiorem exerciturum. Ob quod sibi caucius providendum et aliquid ex adverso opertere conari, quo sua roborata, pars adversarii debilitaretur. Inito ergo consilio, cunctorum in hoc copulatur assensus, ut parvulos, filium scilicet et filiam (F. f. 4r, col. 2) regis Caradoci, Griffino auferrent puellamque filio Morovei, ducis Cornubie, in coniugium traderent;[2] quatinus ipsius ducis subsidio puerum, licet decennem, in paternum regnum promovere et Griffino, si quid contra molieretur, possent obsistere.

Inter ceteros autem primores duo, Sadocus et Dunewallus, sibi invicem consanguinei, nobilissimi habebantur proceres, ex quorum sentencia omnium pendebat consilium et qui ipsi conventui presidere videbantur. Hii ex universorum deliberacione

---

1 F. reculimus.
2 F. traderetur.

related before — in fact all the men regarded as certain that King Caradoc had been slain through the conspiracy and design of Griffin his brother. Further, the men, wise by nature, understood that if the support in the kingdom for Griffin and his power should succeed in becoming stronger, the same fate — or worse — which he had ordered for his brother would be ordered for those who remained faithful to him. Considering all this, it was necessary for them to plan ahead with great care and to try to conceal anything important in the plot by which their own forces might be strengthened and the party of the adversary weakened. They formed a plan with which all concurred. They would remove the young son and daughter of King Caradoc from Griffin and arrange a marriage of the princess to the son of Moroveus, Duke of Cornwall, in order that, with the Duke's help, the prince, although ten years old, might gain preferment in his father's kingdom, and they might deter Griffin, should he try anything against them.

Among the other great men of the realm, Sadoc and Dunewall, who were kinsmen, were considered the highest-ranking noblemen. Everyone's views hung upon their words and they themselves appeared to preside over the council. These two, with the agreement of the rest, went to Griffin and demanded

Griffinum adeunt regiosque pueros ab eo reposcunt, a patrie principibus id esse decretum ipsisque placere asserentes, ut parvuli in sua tuicione consisterent, eos ipsi tutarent et educarent, donec etas maturior et hanc nubilem reddisset et puerum ad regni regimina que sibi iure debebantur admitteret. Sic pacem firmandam, patrie concordiam futuram, principum nullumque ius regni sibi vendicare ausurum, dum hii in medio consisterent, ad quos regni respiciebat gubernacio.

Tunc Griffinus, licet mente saucius, iram tamen continuit, et, ut erat versute mentis, responsum proceribus distulit, ut, illis in responsi accepcione suspensis, quid adversus eorum conatus sibi utile foret licencius interim provideret. Moxque absque dilacione fidelem nuncium ad nutricium puerorum precipitanter dirigit, eos sibi omni proposita occasione (F. f. 4v) imperans adduci, volens sua sub potestate coherceri, causa quorum sibi periculum timebat imminere. Educabantur autem infantes apud regium venatorem, Ivorium nomine, cuius uxor, Morwen dicta, ipsos gemellos gemino lactaverat ubere. Ipsos autem pueros tante pulcritudinis gracia venustabat, ut ultra mortale

from him as a right the custody of the royal children, declaring it to be the decree of the lords of the kingdom, with their approval, that the children should dwell under their care and protection. They would be their guardians and their teachers till more mature years should restore and admit this marriageable princess and young prince to the throne for reigns owed them by law. Thus peace should be secured and the unity of the country established for the future, for no nobleman would dare to arrogate to himself the authority of kingship while these two remained in the custody of the lords to whom the governance of the kingdom belonged.

Then Griffin, though inwardly affronted, controlled his wrath, and as he was cunning, he delayed his reply to the lords, leaving them in suspense regarding his response, so that he might plan meanwhile what action might be taken in his own interest against the efforts of these men. And then without delay he sent a loyal messenger to go immediately to the man responsible for the rearing of the children, ordering them brought to him on any opportune pretense. What he desired was to hold them under his personal control because he feared imminent danger to himself from the children. They were being reared by the royal master of the hunt, Ivor by name, whose wife Morwen had nursed the twins at her own two breasts. The grace of such beauty adorned

quiddam (R. p. 96) in eis relucere crederes. Puer autem Meriadocus, puella vero[1] Orwen dicebatur.

Ivorius, igitur, mandato Griffini accepto, per nuncium ad se directum parvulos ei destinat, nil mali suspicatus et quid parabatur penitus inscius. Quibus adductis Griffinus consilium init cum suis complicibus, disserens et tractans cum eis quid principum sit obiciendum conatibus. Diversisque diucius inde causis ventilatis, ultima demum in nece puerorum finitur sentencia. Perpendebat enim, quod, si ipsi principibus traderentur, suffragati ipsorum auxilio in se insurgerent, et ut regni heredes, se de regno expellere laborarent. Si vero apud se conservarentur, nichilominus, dum daretur facultas, paternum in se ulcisci niterentur interitum. Atque ita, quia eorum causa se quoquoversus manebat exitium, hinc necessitate cogente, illinc regnandi cupiditate stimulante, eos neci addicendos adiudicat statimque trucidari imperat. Quod ubi infantes eius assis(F. 4v, col. 2)tentes presencie audierunt, lugubri voce in altum emissa, in fletum miserabiliter proruperunt, seque invicem amplexi ad sui avi corruere vestigia, parvisque

1   F. vero *omitted*.

those children that you would think that in them something more than mortal shone forth. The boy was named Meriadoc, the girl Orwen.

Ivor, then, when he had received the order from Griffin, sent the children to him as the messenger had instructed, suspecting no evil and wholly ignorant of what was being secretly planned. When the children had been brought to the court, Griffin began to plot with his accomplices, discussing and persuading them what action should be taken against the efforts of the lords. While various ideas were aired at some length, in the end the consensus was to kill the children. It was all carefully weighed that if they were surrendered by him to the lords, the lords, favored by the support for these children, would rise up against him, and, as heirs of the kingdom, they would work to remove him from the throne; on the other hand, if they were maintained at court, while any possibility remained they would work to avenge on him the death of their father. And so because the outcome would be the same no matter which direction he moved—on this side necessity compelling, on that the lust for absolute power—he sentenced them to be bound over for execution and ordered them slain immediately.

But the little ones, having been admitted into the royal presence, heard everything, began to sob, burst into pitiful wailing, and begged their beloved uncle

manibus eius pedes tenentes, et illis blandis oribus osculantes lacrimabili questu, ac miserandis precibus ut sibi misereretur precabantur. Quis ad hec teneret lacrimas, quis non ad misericordiam flecteretur super tante generositatis alumpnis, super tanto decore preditis, humo stratis, indulgenciam supplicantibus? Griffinus quoque, videns suos nepotes suis provolutos vestigiis, ad misericordiam flectitur, eosque ab intentata cede absolvit. Verumptamen proprie saluti consulens sciensque quod, si salvi evasissent, semper quoquomodo debitas a se penas exigerent, iussit eos ad silvam que Arglud nuncupatur[1] deduci atque laqueo suspendi. Ita tamen ut fragiliori fune, que citius rumpi posset, sibi colla necterentur, fidei sacramento ab xii viris hoc nefas executuris accepto, ut numquam inde discederent, donec rupta corda cecidissent.

Acceptis igitur infantulis, tortores forestam Arglud pecierunt. At ubi ad silvas ventum est, ceperunt mutuo de eorum conqueri exicio, dicentes nefarium esse tam crudeli morte perire quos nihil constabat deliquisse. Motique pietate sic eos statuerunt suspendere, ut et funis cito rumperetur et

---

1   F. nunccupatur.

to have mercy; falling in turn before him, their little hands holding his feet, their innocent lips kissing him, with tearful lament and with pitiable supplications they pleaded that he take pity on them. Who could hold back the tears at this? Who would not be moved to pity over such noble foster children, over such graceful and worthy creatures prostrate and pleading for mercy? Griffin, too, seeing his niece and nephew throw themselves at his feet, was moved to pity and freed them from the intended slaughter. But nevertheless the truth was that when he considered his own safety, knowing that if they escaped unharmed they would unceasingly demand in every possible way the debt he owed in judgment, he ordered them taken to the forest called Arglud and hanged by a noose in such a way that their necks would be tied by a quite thin rope that could be broken quickly. He received the oath of loyalty from twelve men who would carry out this monstrous thing, never leaving that place till at length the ropes broke and they had slaughtered the children.

With the little children in hand, the executioners made for the forest of Arglud. But when they had come to the forest, they began to deplore the necessity of the death of the children, saying to one another that it was evil to execute those known to have never committed a crime. Moved to pity, they decided to hang them in such a way that the rope would break

salvi evadere potuissent. In quodam autem saltu ipsius nemoris annosa quercus a diluvii exstabat tempore, proceritate elata, ramis ampla diffusis, et quam vix bisseni viri brachiorum circumdarent amplexu. Solo tenusque interius erat concava; cuius concavitas in se spaciose viginti contineret homines, adeo artum habens aditum, ut flexo (R. p.97) poplite[1], depressis humeris[2], illam necesse erat subire. Super huius ramum roboris pueros, coniunctis adinvicem vultibus, mutuis inherentes amplexibus, debili fasce[3] illaquearunt, ut, sicut dixi, rupto fune cicius caderent illesisque gutturibus indempnes manerent[4]; citius namque deficiunt qui nexi guttura[5] laqueo suspenduntur. Suspensos autem[6] pueros ipsi econtra, ut sibi imperatum fuerat, observantes residebant.

1 R. poplite *repeated bottom margin marking end of gathering of four sheets.*
2 R. brachiis.
3 R. fune.
4 F. indempni maneret.
5 F. citius ... guttura *omitted.* R. deficiunt *added in scribal hand in margin.*
6 R. vero.

quickly and they would be able to escape safe and sound.

In a certain grove of the same forest an aged oak had stood since the Flood. It had a lofty crown, spreading branches, and a girth which twelve men could scarcely encompass within the reach of their arms. There was a hollow inside up to the lowest branches whose cavity could hold twenty men amply; and this had an opening so small that it was necessary to enter with knees bent and body in a crouched position.

Upon a branch of this oak they hanged the children together with weak binding. They were turned face to face, clinging together with arms entwined, so that, as I have said, when the rope broke quickly, they would fall with throats uninjured, remaining unhurt. (For those who are hanged with a noose around the neck die quickly.) The men stood opposite, observing the hanging children as they had been ordered.

Interea tam tristis rumor ad eorum nutricii Ivorii aures defertur. Que rem sue coniugi, lacrimis suffusus, referens, "Aut" ait, "certe, eos neci surripiam aut una cum eis moriar." Confestimque cornu venatorio collo innexo seque suo cane. Dicto Dolfin, comitante[1] quem multum diligebat, simul cum uxore Morwen ad silvam Arglud iter arripuit, hiis armis tantummodo arcu scilicet cum sagittis et gladio, contentus. Sed quia se solum inermem contra tot intelligebat nil posse valere, industria sanius quam viribus censebat utendum. Quatuor igitur ingentes focos e quatuor partibus ipsius saltus accendit (F. col. 2) accensisque plurimas quas secum attulerat carnes passim iniecit ilicemque[2] vicinam cum coniuge et cane ascendens delituit. Fumo autem ignium per nemoris latitudinem diffuso, ubi lupi in confinio degentes—quorum inibi ingens habebatur copia—odorem perceperunt carnium, illo contendere et confluere ilico[3] ceperunt. Sociisque longius exstantibus diro ululatu, ut moris habent, advocatis, in unius hore spacio pene usque ad duo milia convenere. Adventu quorum illi xii viri nimis perterriti seque videntes tanta luporum hinc et inde obsessos multitudine, dum nec valerent fugere nec loco auderent

1 F. commitante
2 F. illicemque.
3 R. illico.

Meanwhile the tragic news of the children reached the ears of Ivor, their foster father. Relating the situation to his wife, tears streaming, he said, "But surely I can snatch them from death—or else I will die with them." And immediately, the hunting horn still around his neck and his dog Dolfin, which he valued highly, following, together with his wife Morwen he raced for the forest of Arglud.

He was armed only with his bow, arrows, and sword. Because he was alone and without armor against so many men, he knew that he could not prevail, so he resolved to use a strategem, a decision more wise than attempting force. He set four huge fires in the four corners of that grove, and so that they would burn hotter, he threw in randomly the meat that he had brought with him. He, his wife, and the dog climbed into a holly tree close by and hid. The smoke from the fires spread widely through the grove, at the limits of which wolves were lurking. There were a huge number of them there and they smelled the scent of meat. They began to be drawn to it and to converge in that direction. They howled dreadfully as they usually do to alert others of the pack waiting farther away. In less than an hour as many as two thousand had gathered.

Seeing themselves surrounded by so many wolves on every side, the twelve men panicked. Since they

consistere, concavitatem prefate arboris delitescendi gracia omnes subiere.

Lupi autem convenientes rogos catervatim circumstabant[1] atque in flammarum globos ac si inde carnes erepturi impetum faciebant. Tunc Ivorius, tenso arcu, quatuor in illos quatuor ignes vallantes spicula direxit, quatuorque transfossis illiis[2] vulneravit. Sanguine vero effluente, ceteri omnes lupi in eos qui vulnera pertulerant irruerunt eosque[3] membratim dilacerantes discerpserunt. Consuetudinis enim est illis, illo quo ignem perceperint semper[4] contendere, eumque quem e sui numero sauciari contigerit unguibus et dentibus discerpere. Lupis vero circa rogos certantibus et tumultuantibus, cavee inclusis metus augebatur (F. f. 5v)[5] lupos sui causa circa quercum exterius sevire reputantibus.[6] Ad hec Ivorius cornu horribliter[7] insonuit eiusque strepitu universos inde lupos abegit. Nichil enim adeo lupi quam sagittas et tubarum metuunt strepitum. Unde eciam raro aut numquam venatoribus lesionem (R. p. 98) inferunt.

1 F. circumastabant.
2 R. iliis.
3 R. illosque.
4 R. semper *omitted.*
5 *Sentence division in R at page turn in F.*
6 R. *paragraph marker.*
7 F. horibiliter.

could not flee nor did they dare remain where they were, they all scrambled into the hollow of the tree to hide.

The wolves, meanwhile, gathering in packs, surrounded the balefires and made forays at the raging flames, trying to snatch the meat. Then Ivor, drawing his bow, shot darts into those animals at the fires and wounded four. Attracted by the streaming blood, the rest of the wolves attacked the wounded ones and mangled them, tearing them limb from limb. (For it is typical of wolves to contend for dominance over a fire, and with claws and fangs they rip apart those of their number already wounded.) While the wolves struggled and fought around the fires, the terror of those shut up within the hollow tree grew. They realized that when the wolves sensed their plight, the packs would ravin outside the oak.

At this point, Ivor sounded an unnerving blast on his horn; the shock drove all the wolves away. (For wolves fear nothing so much as arrows and the blast of the horn and consequently they rarely ever attack hunters.)

Ivorius igitur inde, lupis abactis, arborem qua considerat descendit ac[1] ignem copiosum ante ipsius fovee introitum qua viri latebant cumulavit; cuius calore fumique vapore inclusos pene extinxit. Illi autem se interius quantum valebant retrahebant et artabant, sed Ivorius nichilominus semper ignem propius[2] admovens insequebatur, donec sub ipso ore spelunce flammam ingessit. Tunc illi torridi et semiusti una voce, "Ivori, miserere!" exclamant, "scimus enim quis sis et quod causa parvulorum hoc in nos sis machinatus discrimen.[3] Sed, quesumus, ignem a nobis[4] amove et facultatem hinc egrediendi tribue; et nos tecum pueris liberum paciemur[5] abire." Quibus Ivorius: "Exite, ergo." Ignemque e latere hinc et inde amovens, exeundi facultatem dedit. Erat autem, ut in anterioribus retuli, ipsius cavee aditus tam artus et summissus, ut non nisi unum solum intrantem vel exeuntem et illum flexo poplite, capite demisso, admitteret et emitteret. Data itaque exeundi licencia, unus solus repens manibus et pedibus egreditur. Qui cum cervicem extulisset, Ivorius a foris e latere spelunce consistens, evaginato gladio, ei caput[6] amputavi. Truncumque[7] ad se cadaver

1 R. ac *omitted.*
2 F. & R. proprius.
3 R. crimen.
4 R. amove *in margin.*
5 R. patiemur.
6 F. capud.
7 F. trunccumque.

Ivor then, having driven off the wolves, climbed down from the tree in which he had taken his post. He heaped a huge fire before the entrance to the hollow where the men had crawled. It almost smothered those inside with its heat, smoke, and fumes. They succeeded in drawing further in and closer together, but Ivor still kept after them, always pushing the fire closer till he forced the flame under the mouth of the cavity itself. Then parched and half-burnt, they screamed as one, "Ivor, have mercy! We know for certain it is you and that you have devised this trap for us to save the children. But we beg you, if you will push the fire away from us and give us a chance to get out of here, we swear that the children may go free with you." To this Ivor replied, "Come out then." And moving the fire aside, he gave them a chance to get out.

The access to that opening, as I have related previously, was so narrow and low that in order for even one person alone to come in or go out, he had to bend his knees and duck his head. Permission to come out having been granted, one man by himself, creeping on hands and feet, made his way to the exit. When he had stuck his neck out, Ivor, standing to the side of the opening, drew his sword and cut off his head. And

extrahens, "Exite hinc! propere hinc," exclamat, "exite! Quid moramini?" Unus igitur post unum omnes[1] egressi sunt, singulisque egredientibus Ivorius caput[2] abscidit.

Hiis ita gestis, pueros iam[3] pene dimidie diei suspensos[4] spacio, eciam fere exanimes, deposuit, allatoque cibo eorum animas parum refocillavit, ac deinde cum eis et suo cane Dolfin et coniuge ad silvam Fleventanam[5] confugit. Verebatur namve propter Griffini furorem[6] vel domum redire vel quoquam in patria clam amplius consistere. In illa autem silva rupes[7] ardua nimis eminebat, rupe[8] aquilarum nuncupata,[9] eo quod omni tempore quatuor super illam nidificient aquile, contra quatuor principales ventos semper vultus converse habentes. Et ipsa vero et in ipsa rupe aula perampla, perpulcri thalami, diversaque miri operis ad insta testudinis erant incisa edificia, habitacula ciclopum olim credita, sed ante illud tempus

1   R. omnes *added above the line..*
2   F. capud.
3   R. fere.
4   R. spacio suspensos.
5   R. eleventanam.
6   F. furo-rorem, *syllable doubled when the word was divided.* R. fuororem.
7   F. rupis.
8   F. rupis.
9   F. nunccupata.

pulling the body on out, he shouted, "Come on, hurry up! Get on out of there! What's holding you up?" One after the other they each attempted to get out, and one after another, Ivor decapitated them.

When this was done, he lifted the children down. They had already been suspended for nearly half a day and seemed lifeless. He refreshed their spirits somewhat by giving them a little food, and then he fled with them, along with his dog Dolfin and his wife, to the forest of Fleventan. Knowing the fury of Griffin, he was afraid to return home or to remain hidden any longer within the kingdom.

In that forest, however, an extremely steep cliff rises called the "cliff of the eagles" where at all times four eagles build their nests high on it, turning their faces always into the four directions of the winds. And in this very cliff are a great cavern, a very beautiful chamber, and various other hollowed-out rooms, with marvelous structures hanging from what is the roof of the cave. It is believed to have been at one time the dwelling place of the Cyclopes, but since that age it has scarcely been seen by anyone, concealed as it is in the depths of that hidden and extremely dense forest.

vix ab aliquo comperta, archano et densissimo nemoris sinu recondita. Hec edificia Ivorius cum infantulis peciit, ac ibi quinquennio omnibus incognitus moram fecit. Ferina caro quam venatu conquirebat cibum, latex haustum prebebat. Nuces quoque pomaque silvestria et ceteri fructus qui inibi inveniri poterant, autump(F. f. 6r)nali collecti tempore et reconditi, alimento serviebant. Ivorius cum Meriadoco venatum et aucupatum cotidie pergebat; Morwen vero, uxor eius, puella Orwen secum assumpta, in colligendo fructus vel herbas occupabatur.

Set hic fortassis queritur quomodo sibi carnes ad esum paraverint, dum et ignis et vasa quibus elixari possent defuerint. Carnes quidem sibi pabula(R. p. 99)tum more silvis exulancium accurare consueverant. Huiusmodi quippe homines prediis vel patria scelere exigente expulsi, publica ab conversacione remocius semoti, saltus silvarumque latebras usque frequentantes, dum vasis cibis elixandis necessariis indigent, ignem silice[1] eliciunt, piram quam maximam e[2] sarmentorum lignorumque constructam congeri

1 R. cilice.
2 R. ex.

Ivor made for this chambered cavern with the little ones, and they remained there utterly hidden for five years. Game, which he sought by hunting, provided food, and water drink. They were able to find wild fruits and nuts, and other green things which could be eaten. Gathered in the fall and stored, these served for winter provisions. Ivor pursued hunting and fowling with Meriadoc daily; his wife Morwen, taking the young Orwen with her, worked at gathering fruits and herbs.

But it may be asked how they prepared the meat for food for themselves when they lacked both fire and pots in which it could be cooked. Yet they did have ways to prepare game for their nourishment while exiled in the forest, just as outlaws, forced to flee because of crimes against estate or country, now removed far from the normal way of life and hiding out in the deep woods and forests, survive without vessels necessary for cooking food. These men build a great structure of brushwood and logs, strike fire from flint, and light the pile from the top. When this has

e copiose accendunt; accenseque caucium quot voluerint[1] calefaciendos iniciunt. Interim vero ceteri, terram cavantes, binas fossas non eiusdem quantitatis preparant, una quarum alta et ampla, altera parum arcior et profundior exstat. Sicque constituuntur ad invicem, ut semipedis inconvulse terre spacium inter eas maneat. Per illud autem spacium a maiori ad humiliorem foveam fit oblique haud[2] magnum foramen quod clepsedra[3] vel sude obturatur. Inde unda implent maiorem. Carnes vero elixandas in minori collocant, viridi quoquoversus substrato gramine, locatasque iterum herba cooperiunt. (F. f. 6v, col. 2) Hiis autem ita compositis, iam[4] scintillantes foco eiectos caudices in foveam repletam devolvunt latice.[5] Ab quorum fervore limpha non solum estuans sed eciam ebulliens, dempta clusilla,[6] in continenti pabula[7] percurrere[8] cavea sinitur. Hocque[9] tam diu fit donec sufficienter elixa caro extrahatur.[10] Ivorius, quoque, eo ordine carnes elixandas conficiens, cibum sibi gratissimum et saporissimum accurabat. Attritis autem et consumptis vestimentis que illuc attulerant,

1 R. volverunt.
2 F. haut.
3 R. clipsedra.
4 F. iam *added above line.*
5 F. lance.
6 R. dusilla.
7 R. *added in margin.*
8 R. procurrere.
9 R. Hoc itaque.
10 R. retrahatur.

burned down, they throw on as many rocks as they want to be heated. Meanwhile, other men, hollowing out the earth, prepare a pair of pits of different sizes, one deep and wide, the other a little narrower but deeper. These are laid out alongside each other so that a space of about six inches of undisturbed earth separates them. Through this space a drain runs at an angle from the larger to the shallower pit, not too large but that it can be closed with a sort of valve or spike. Then they fill the larger one with water. They place meat wrapped in green leaves, ready to be boiled, in the smaller, and they cover the food so prepared with even more herbs. When this has been properly arranged, they roll the blocks of wood already glowing on the fire base into the pit full of water. From these the water not only becomes hot but actually boils up. With the closing device wide open, the water is allowed to run off into the pit containing the food. This process is continued for as long as it takes for the meat to be thoroughly cooked.

Ivor, preparing boiled meat in this way, provided for them all food that was both thoroughly satisfying and quite delicious. When the clothes that they brought with them wore out, they wove for themselves garments of reeds and sewed together the leaves of trees.

indumenta sibi[1] ex papiris[2] texuerunt ac arborum consuerunt foliis.

E menso vero v annorum spacio, quadam die, dum nemus se solito spatiatum lustrarent et Morwen cum puella longius ab Ivorio esset semota, ecce Urianus cum Kaio, regis Arturi dapifero, media via illis occurrit. Urianus vero rex erat Scocie curiamque regis Arturi adierat, eumque ad propria repedantem Kaius iussu regis Arturi conducebat. Cumque simul properantes cominus puelle devenissent, salutans sibi invicem Kaius quidem regreditur: Urianus vero ceptum iter prosequitur. Qui puellam eleganti forma contemplatus, tanteque esse pulcritudinis, quante nunquam aliquam noverat, ipsius amore succenditur. Illo equum convertit; illam nequicquam reluctantem ante se super sonipedem sustulit, ac, nutrice flente relicta, suam in patriam abduxit.

K ayus[3] quoque, dum per artam semitam (F. f. 6r) in[4] regrediendo tenderet, Ivorium et Meriadocum venatu honustos[5] obvios habuit. Ipseque incomparabilem pueri admiratus speciem — erat enim

1 R. sibi *precedes* texuerunt.
2 F. pappiris.
3 F. Gaius.
4 F. in *omitted.*
5 R. onustos.

After five years had passed, a day came that while, as their custom was, they had gone out to scour the forest, and Morwen and Orwen were some distance from Ivor, it so happened that Urien with Kay, seneschal for King Arthur, came upon them in the middle of the roadway. Urien was, in fact, King of Scotland, and he had gone to the court of King Arthur. Sir Kay, under Arthur's orders, was escorting him on his return to his own country. Since they were moving along together in some haste, after they had come upon the young woman, Kay exchanged farewells and turned back. Urien, then, continued along the route they had been following. He thought about the girl, about her graceful bearing, about her beauty which was beyond that of any woman he had ever known, and he was set afire with love for her. He turned his horse about and snatched up the girl on it, even though she struggled. He carried the girl away into his own country, leaving the nurse screaming behind.

Kay, while returning along the narrow path, confronted Ivor and Meriadoc, who were laden with game from hunting. Kay, marveling at the splendid beauty of the youth — for he was fair-haired,

flavis capillis, nitida facie, procera statura et pectore exstante, ilibus gracilioribus — cornipedem post ipsos iam fugientes admittit, Ivorioque longius terrore abacto, Meriadocum rapuit ovansque secum devexit.

Ivorius autem, erepto sibi puero Meriadoco, sua lugubris (R. p.100) habitacula repetit, quo suam[1] coniugem similem deflentem querelam offendens quod discrimen incurrerant alterutro referunt. Pro quo infortunio eiusmodi dolor eorum mentes occupavit, ut continuo[2] bienno post amissionem puerorum se inmitigabili luctu torquentes non sine maxima cibi potusque penuria inibi soli degerent.

Expleto vero biennio, dum una die[3] se conquerentes invicem multa conferrent, "Quid," ait illa, "hic solitarii degimus? Causa puerorum huc confugimus, ut eos vite conservaremus, hic hactenus[4] perstitimus; quibus ablatis et desideratis, quid hic nos ulterius detinet? Saniori profecto uteremur consilio, si quo abducti sint inquirere et indagare studuissemus. Pergam certe nunquam indultura labori, nunquam

---

1   F. sua.
2   F. ut continuo *added above line*.
3   F. dierum.
4   R. actenus.

handsome, tall, broad-chested, and quite lithe of body—spurred his horse after the two fugitives. When he had driven Ivor away in terror, Kay took Meriadoc captive and, rejoicing, carried him off with him.

Ivor, having had Meriadoc taken from him, returned mournfully to his cave shelter, where, finding his wife likewise grief-stricken, they told one another about the terrible catastrophes that had befallen them. The pain of these misfortunes so distressed them that for two years after the loss of the children, tormenting themselves with unremitting sorrow, they lived on in that solitary place, not without great scarcity of food and drink.

A full two years had passed when one day while they were commiserating over what had happened, the woman said,"Why do we remain alone here in this solitary place? We took refuge here on behalf of the children in order to save their lives; till now we have remained here. But since they have been carried off and we grieve for them, why do we stay here any longer? It seems wiser indeed to make some plan, so that we might undertake a thorough search for them and track down the paths where they have been taken.

captura quietem, donec puellam michi surreptam usquam fortuna nancisci[1] con(F. f. 6v, col. 2)cesserit. Scio autem quod hac parte et manum contra boream tetendit abducta sit. Miles enim[2] qui virum conducebat, a quo puella rapta est, dum ab eo discederet, se in Scociam ad eum[3] venturum promisit eique proprio valedicens nomine Urianum nuncupavit." Ivorius: "Ego quidem curiam regis Arturi frequenter frequentavi, ei venatorio officio obsequens, quo, si umquam Kaius ipsius dapifer michi visus et conitus est, illum[4] a me puerum Meriadocum abstulisse non dubito. Ibo et ego, si forte divinum numen, nostri miseratum doloris, eum michi aliquorsum obtulerit." Dicta faciunt; se mutuo flentes osculantur; diversasque vias ineuntes ab invicem dirimuntur. .

Morwen igitur ad Scociam iter arripuit; ipsaque die qua Urianus rex, puella Orwen sibi in uxore dotata, celebres nupcias agebat, illo pervenit. Iam namque Orwen nubilem etatem attigerat; et quibus erat oriunda natalibus, ipsa referente, Uriano regi evidenter patuerat. Missarum autem peractis solempniis,[5] dum

1 F. nanccissci.
2 R. vero.
3 R. se.
4 R. ipsium.
5 R. solemniis.

I will steadfastly refuse to know any pleasure or find any rest till Fortuna grants that the girl taken from me is found, wherever she may be. I know for a fact that she was carried off in that direction, toward the north. What is more, when the knight who was leading the man by whom the girl was kidnapped parted from him, he promised he would come to him in Scotland, and he called out his name 'Urien' in farewell."

Ivor said, "On many occasions in my office as huntsman I have been in King Arthur's court where I often saw and recognized Kay the Seneschal, and I do not doubt that it was he who stole the boy from me. I myself will go to see if by chance the Divine Goddess, having mercy on our grief, will grant that I find him, wherever he is." Having said this, weeping, they kissed one another and set out to go their separate ways.

Morwen then took the road to Scotland; on the very day that she arrived, King Urien had taken the girl Orwen as his bride and the well-attended wedding was ending. For now Orwen had reached the marriageable age, and when her birthday came she had made it known clearly to King Urien, she herself informing him. When high mass had been celebrated,

regina Orwen splendidis ornata indumentis ab ecclesia ad palacium rediret, Morwen, turbis pauperum qui elemosinam petituri confluerant inmixta, ipsam[1] quidem diligenter contemplabatur, set eam minime cognoscere potuit. Ex varietate quippe cultus sepe fallitur cognicio vultus.[2] (F. f. 7r) At regina inter catervas pauperum parum subsistens, cui bonus mos inoleverat egenos semper fovere et eorum inopiam sua supplere habundancia, dum pietatis in eos intuitum flecteret, suam nutricem inopinate advertit, animadversamque cognovit. Quam statim ut aspexit, pallore suffunditur et tum dolore preteritorum, tum gaudio presencium, mente sibi evanescente, in mentis excessum rapitur ac inter manus procerum quibus incumbebat ad terram labitur. Ad hec nobiles et proceres omnesque circumstantes obstupefacti accurrunt. Adest et ipse rex Urianus nimis trepidus, eamque in se reversam relevans[3] quid habuisset (R. p. 101) interrogat. Regina, "Non est mirum, domine," respondit, "si vultus. palluerit, si mens mihi defecerit — mihi me coram illam intuenti assistere que cum maximo proprio dispendio me neci surripuit et usque ad etatem adultam educavit. Set nunc quam cara tibi habear, quo me amore diligas, in ea ostendere poteris. Quia quicquid[4] boni vel honoris illi

1 R. ipsamque.
2 F. *bracketed in margin as a sententia*.
3 F. revelans.
4 R. quidquid.

Queen Orwen, splendidly gowned, was returning from the church to the palace. Morwen, crowded in by the paupers who had gathered to seek alms, viewed her carefully, but was not able in the least to recognize her. (With a great change of attire it is often difficult to recognize a face.) But the queen, standing a little back among the crowds of beggars, had developed the good custom to always favor the poor, and turning her gaze of pity upon them, she supplied their lack from her abundance. Unexpectedly her eyes fell upon her nurse and she recognized her. As she realized the truth of what she saw, she immediately turned pale, now from the pain of the remembered past, now from the joy of the present. Her consciousness faded and she fell into a faint, and from the hands of the noblemen on whom she was leaning she sank to the ground.

The lords and nobles and all those standing in attendance were stunned and rushed to her. King Urien himself was there and, greatly frightened, he lifted her toward him and asked what had happened. The queen replied, "It isn't surprising, my lord, if my face paled or if I became faint when I saw the woman who snatched me from death at great sacrifice to herself and even raised me from infancy to adulthood. How dear I am to you, by what love you cherish me, you now can show through her. For whatever benefit

impenderis, me gracius accepturam[1] quam mihimet impensum cognoscito." Suamque nutricem medio pauperum evocans, lacrimis prorumpentibus, eius collo brachia iniecit ac ante regem Urianum papira dumtaxat veste amictam statuit. Urianus vero, liberalitatem laudans coniugis, iussit Morwen thalamo induci, optimo cultu indui, omniaque ei reperiens necessaria, cum regina fecit morari.

Ivorius autem interea regis Arturi curiam adiit, atque eo convivante, cuius fores nunquam tempore prandii claudebantur, regiam aulam, omnibus spectaculo factus subiit. Vir namque innormis proceritatis erat, torva facie, barba prolixa, incultis crinibus, scyrpis et papiris[2] contextis amictus, ense latus cinctus, venatorium cornu collo, arcum cum sagittis manu, cervum vero exanimem magni ponderis inmenseque magnitudinis, quem sibi obvium casu venatu ceperat, humeris gestans. Regiam autem ingressus, universos hinc et inde discumbentes diucius immobilis persistens diligenti cepit perlustrari lumine, si forte quempiam inter eos cognosceret, a quo et ipse quis esset innotesci valerat, set neminem preter Kaium dapiferum advertit quem sibi antea cognitum

---

[1] R. accepturum.
[2] R. et cirpis et papiris.

and honor you bestow upon this woman will be appreciated by me more gratefully than if bestowed on me." Summoning the nurse from the midst of the beggars, with a flood of tears she threw her arms around her neck; and the nurse, wrapped in a garment of woven reed fibers, stood before the king. Urien, praising the generosity of his bride, ordered Morwen to be taken to a chamber, to be attired in the best fashion, and supplying all her needs, had her remain with the queen.

Ivor, meanwhile, arrived at King Arthur's court and, as the king was feasting and the gates were never closed during the serving, he entered the royal hall, making a spectacle for all to behold. He was a man indeed of enormous height, stern face, bushy beard, uncut hair, and he was clothed in woven reeds and fibers, with a sword belted at his side, a hunting horn around his neck, bow and arrows in his hand, and across his shoulders the carcass of a huge and heavy deer which he had slain on the way. When he had entered the palace, he stopped and stood for a long time, and with a shrewd eye he began to scrutinize all those reclining, from those close by to those on the far side of the hall, to see if by chance he might recognize someone among them by whom he himself might succeed in being identified. But he saw no one except Kay the Seneschal, whom he recognized from having

recognoscebat. Quo viso, ceteris pretergressis,
confestim coram eo ad mensam accessit, eum
salutavit, suoque prolato vocabulo et quis esset
ostenso, cervum eius ante pedes deposuit, ut sui
munusculum non dedignaretur accipere rogitans.
Meriadocus vero, Ivorio intrante, mense cum aliis
residens, ut eum conspexit, quis erat falli non potuit,
confestimque[1] iunctis pedibus mensam transsiliit, in
eius amplexus lacrimis suffusus irruit, eum necis
liberatorem viteque conservatorem contestans et
clamitans. Deinde cum eo ante Kaium accedens
dapiferum, (F. f. 7v) commemoratis ab eo sibi
collocatis beneficiis, ut illius dignaretur, sui gracia,
remunerare benivolenciam suppliciter exorabat.
Kaius, autem,[2] non ignarus quis esset, quippe qui sibi
quondam multociens suo solebat obsequi officio,
precipue tamen gracia Meriadoci, illum penes se
retinuit ac quibus indigebat liberaliter ditavit.

Non multum post hoc[3] temporis effluxerat et Kaius
dapifer, ut ipsum Uriano spopondisse
commemoravimus, in Scociam proficiscitur, Ivorium et
Meriadocum secum adducens. Bellorum quippe

---

1   F. que *added above line.*
2   R. vero.
3   R. hec.

known him before. When Ivor had seen him, he passed by all the others, and at once approached him at the table, greeted him openly, and after he had told him his name and revealed who he was, he laid the deer before Kay's feet so that he might not scorn to hear the request he was making. Meriadoc, at Ivor's entrance, was reclining at dinner with the others; when he saw him, he could not mistake who he was, and immediately he put his feet together and leaped over the table. He rushed into his arms, weeping, testifying, and proclaiming how Ivor had rescued him from certain death and had kept him alive. Then coming with him before Sir Kay the Seneschal, he told the story of all the good that Ivor had done for him, asking that in return Kay would consider him worthy to be granted the kindness he humbly requested. Kay, however, not ignorant of who he was — in fact Ivor had served him as huntsman in the past on many occasions — but chiefly on account of the gratitude of Meriadoc, received him into his service and supplied him richly with what he needed.

Not long afterward, Kay the Seneschal, in accordance with the promise already recounted that he had made to Urien, began the journey to Scotland, taking Ivor and Meriadoc with him. He had not been

impedimentis instantibus quibus sub rege Arturo semper[1] occupabatur nunquam antea expediri potuit, ut secundum suam promissionem, illo proficisci valuissset. In Scociam igitur ad regem Uranium pervenientes, ultra (R. p. 102) omnem[2] estimacionem Ivorius uxorem, Meriadocus sororem suam sanam et[3] hilarem, ingentique honore et gloria[4] preditam reperit. Quantum hinc eis exoritur gaudium, quam efficax preteritorum sibi hinc evenerit remedium, ex ipsius rei eventu perpendere[5] poteris. Que enim maior leticia quam parentes[6] et amici tristes divcius divisi se tandem hillares reperire, post nimios labores potiri quiete, pauperiemque et miseriam divitiis et gloria commutare? Universos igitur commune gaudium optinet, plurimi in deliciis dies ob tantam Fortune graciam ab eis continuantur preteritique dolores relevantur gaudiis.[7]

---

1   R. semper *omitted.*
2   R. omen.
3   R. incolumen *before* hilarem.
4   R. et gloria *in margin, scribal hand.*
5   F. prependere.
6   F. perentes.
7   R. gaudiis relevantur. F. gaudiis *added by different hand.*

able to go as he had promised any earlier because of his responsibility for keeping Arthur's battle supplies in constant readiness. In Scotland, coming before King Urien, beyond all expectation, Ivor found his wife, Meriadoc his sister—safe, happy, and held in great honor and respect.

You may judge from the outcome what great joy rose up for them, what a sovereign remedy for the past thus had come about. What greater joy is there than for grieving parents or friends separated for a long time to find themselves joyfully together again, or after great effort to find rest, or to see poverty and suffering changed to riches and glory? The joy was shared by all; they continued in delight for many days through the great grace of Fortuna, and the grief of the past was lightened by joy.

Cum autem simul inibi[1] commorarentur, ceperunt sui patrui Griffini nequiciam, quam tum in suo genitore, tum et in se nequiter exercuerat, crebro sermone revolvere et si aliquo modo vicem sue malicie illi reddere valerent propensius agere. Sed, quia regem Arturum illi favere non ignorabant, sub cuius Griffinus degebat[2] imperio, sibi minime successurum sciebant, si sine regis Arturi assensu et auxilio aliquid in eum moliri conarentur. Ex communi igitur sentencia et deliberacione oportunum tempus nacti, regem Arturum super hiis se apud eum conquesturi[3] adeunt. A quo honorificie suscepti causam adventus insinuant, flebili querimonia rem gestam ei per ordinem referunt, et ut se super tanto ulcisceretur[4] scelere illius genibus provoluti suppliciter deposcunt. Rex autem Arturus regis quondam[5] Caradoci probitatem et sapienciam ad memoriam reducens et tam inauditum Griffini detestans[6] facinus ei confestim misso mandavit nuncio, ut die statuta ad suam veniret curiam, super fratricidio quod sibi imponebatur responsurus..

1 R. inibi simul.
2 R. vivebat.
3 F. conquturi, *corrected above line.*
4 F. uscisceretur.
5 F. quodam.
6 F. distans.

While they remained in Urien's court together, they met frequently to deliberate about the crimes of King Griffin, their uncle, because he had devised evil against not only their father but also themselves. If they could in some way be strong enough to requite this injury, they would take action most willingly. But because they were not unaware that King Arthur favored Griffin, and Griffin dwelt within Arthur's writ, they knew they would have little success if they attempted to move against him without the consent and aid of Arthur. As a result of their common decision and deliberation, having chosen an opportune time, they went before King Arthur to place their case against Griffin. Received by the King with honor, they pleaded the cause for which they had come and presented the facts of what had happened in proper order, a grievance worthy of tears. Falling on their knees, they requested humbly that he grant them vengeance for this man's great crime. King Arthur, holding to the memory of the probity and wisdom of the deceased King Caradoc and so execrating the crime of which Griffin was accused but not yet tried, ordered immediately a summons sent him by messenger that on the day decreed he should appear in Arthur's court in order to defend himself concerning the fratricide of which he had been accused.

Griffinus vero hactenus fama vulgante suos nepotes quos neci addixerat audito evasisse, semper habens suspectum se non impune laturum scelus quod in eos orsus fuerat, locis opportunis castella condiderat; virisque et pabulo in preparacionem pugne callide sufficienter munierat. Et (F. f. 8r) maxime nivalem montem qui Kambrice[1] Snawdown dicitur,[2] situ loci ceteris tuciorem, munire curavit, quem quasi asilum constituit omnibus eciam incolis cum parvulis et mulieribus et sua supellectili[3] universa super eum tuto abductis et collocatis. Quibus rebus Griffinus confisus destinato sibi ab rege Arturo nuncio se nequaquam ad eius curiam[4] respondit venturum, unde Arturus nimium commotus, instructa militum copia, cum Uriano rege Scocie contra eum ilico ascendit.

Griffinus vero, cognito ipsius adventu, omnes viarum transitus quibus Kambria adibatur[5] antea obstruxerat, una sola relicta pervia, que hinc et inde imminencium rupium tam artis arcebatur faucibus, uti

---

1   R. *uses the "C" spelling frequently but not consistently.*
2   F. Snaudune dictum.
3   F. supplectili.
4   F. curriam, *corrected.*
5   F. adiebatur.

Griffin, in fact, had already heard the rumors now widely circulating that the niece and nephew whom he had sentenced to death had escaped. This man, who had always felt that he would not escape with impunity the crime he had attempted against them, had built fortresses in strategic places and, with appropriate foresight, had readied them with men and provisions in preparation for war. He had taken care to fortify to the fullest extent the snow-peaked mountain which the Cambrians call Snowdon, a site more secure than the others, which he had set up as a place of refuge for all the inhabitants with their women and children, as well as his entire possessions. These had been assembled and brought up the mountain to safety. Griffin, confident because of his preparations, replied to the messenger from King Arthur that he would by no means come to his court. Extremely disturbed by his reply, Arthur allied himself with Urien of Scotland and moved against Griffin as quickly as his troops could be equipped and supplied.

In truth, Griffin, knowing that he would come, had already blockaded all the roads by which Cambria could be invaded. Only one route remained, on either side of which great cliffs towered, a defile so narrow it would allow the passage of only one traveler at a time

non nisi unum post alium viatorem caperet. Hanc quoque ipse Griffinus, armatorum stipatus catervis, obsidens, regem Arturum inibi, nusquam alias reperto transeundi aditu, meare conantem facili repellebat iniuria. Quo dum Arturus, nescius quid faceret, (R. p.103) in transeundo moras necteret, Sadocus et Dunewallus — illi duo proceres quos a Griffino pueros petisse superius ostendimus — collecta et conducta valida mulitudine militum, inprovisi parte alia in illius irrupere[1] provinciam flammaque et cede nulli parcentes etati quoquoversus depopulabantur. Cuius rei Griffinus, percepto nuncio, suis pereuntibus succursum[2] ire contendens, vallem quam (F. col. 2) obsederat[3] incustoditam reliquit, aciemque contra duos prefatos proceres direxit. Sicque, libero Arturo patefacto introitu, omnem statim illas Scilleas fauces traiecit exercitum, Griffinumque insecutus in quodam op[p]ido preardua rupe constructo obsedit, erectisque in circuitu aggeribus, inpugnare cepit. Fecerunt et ipsi machinas contra machinas, seque viriliter propugnantes fortiter restiterunt. Horum extrinsecus iuges fiebant assultus; illi econtra cotidie subitos in

---

1 R. prorupere.
2 R. succursurum.
3 R. obsiderat.

Griffin himself, supported by a troop of armored men, defended this pass. When King Arthur, finding no other way to invade Cambria, attempted to get through, Griffin's attack blocked him easily. While Arthur, knowing no other route, was delayed in invading, Sadoc and Dunewall (those two lords who, as we have shown earlier, had petitioned to get the children away from Griffin) had recruited and organized a significant number of knights to revolt against Griffin. Those knights rose up without warning in another part of the kingdom, wreaking havoc by fire and sword and sparing no one whatsoever for age. When the messengers brought news of this, Griffin, constrained to go to the aid of his imperiled people, left the valley which he had held without a garrison and led his army against those two lords.

And as soon as Arthur was free to move and the pass lay open to him, the entire army immediately began to file through that Scyllean chasm, pursuing Griffin to the fortress built in his mountain fastness. Arthur laid siege, and building emplacements for his war machines round about, he began the assault. They in turn set their machines against those machines, and fighting bravely and fiercely they held their ground. These men made constant sallies outside the walls; from the other side, they mounted sudden attacks against them every day.

eos moliebantur[1] excursus. Modo telorum balistarumque iactus eminus precrebrescere,[2] modo congressiones militum cominus videres fervescere; modo distinctis aciebus dextrisque consertis in mutuam cedem adverse irruebant caterve, resque maximo agebatur discrimine.

At rex Arturus, loci posicione diligencius inspecta, que suimet natura eciam absque propugnatore valde muniebatur — una namque tantum ex parte, in ipso declivi montis latere, difficilime ascendebatur, tantaque erecta celsitudine, ut vix ad ipsius culmen telorum iactus pertingeret — perpendensque inclusorum excursibus municipii capiundi dilacionem fieri, eos artius propensiusque expungnare statuit. Fossam igitur amplam et profundam ante ipsas valvas oppidi ducere precipit, ut et eorum refrenaret excursus et, si viribus non posset, vel eos fame ad dedicionem[3] cogeret. (F. f. 8v) Deinde per girum, silva succisa, aggeres quam plurimi hinc et inde eriguntur, unde crebri[4] iactus volvebantur lapidum iaculacionesque agebantur

1   F. molliebantur.
2   R. percrebescere
3   F. dediconem.
4   R. crebi.

You could see how the showers of spears and missiles were hurled from afar, how the knights fought heated encounters close in, how opposing formations of foot soldiers fought hand to hand with mounted troops in mutual slaughter, and how the battle was waged to the death.

But King Arthur examined the situation of the fortress more carefully, seeing that it was secure by its very nature even without its walls: on the one hand, because of the very declivity of the mountain, it could be approached only with very great difficulty, and on the other, because of its elevation, the range of his missiles was scarcely adequate. And considering the time it would take to reduce the fortress by siege, he decided to subdue them with more stringent and more deliberate measures. Therefore he advised a deep and wide fosse to be extended before the very walls of the fortress, so that not only could he stop their sallies, but also (if not by force of arms, at least because of hunger) he might coerce them to surrender. Finally, felling timber in the surrounding forest, he erected even higher emplacements on every side from which frequent volleys of stones were hurled and missiles were launched.

missilium. Ad hec Griffinus, obsidionem artatam totumque advertens negocium in virtute consistere, singulis quibusque eorum machinamentis contraria obiciebat, omni elaborns conamine, ut nequaquam ascribi valeret inercie, si sese quoquomodo devinci contigisset.[1] Ratum tamen habebat, se nullius viribus nisi sola fame submittendum. Quod et ita provenit. Toto namque triennio semper hostibus invinicibilis restitit, donec victrix vincencium ei nimia fames ingruit, que citius omni robore mentes robustorum flectere et ad dedicionem solet compellere. Quid ultra? Famis peste ingruente Griffinus conpulsus se in regis Arturi misericordia dedidit. Arturus autem se de eo misericordiam habiturum negavit, nisi suorum parium iudicio procerum. Iussu igitur regis Arturi proceres ad iudicium exeunt, quorum censura eum capitali addixit sentencie. Iniustum namque omnibus videbatur, illum diucius vivere, quem tantum facinus in fratrem et nepotes constabat commississe. Data itaque sentencia, deo eius ultore nequicie, Griffinus capite plectitur.

1   F. contigesset.

At this, Griffin, observing the hemming-in tactics and realizing that the entire affair rested on valor, concentrated on the emplacements of war machines one by one, undertaking this with great effort, so that in no way would it be attributed to cowardice if he were somehow defeated. He was determined that he would be overcome by no force save hunger alone. And so it turned out: he withstood the enemy for three whole years, ever invincible, until a great, all-conquering hunger assailed that unconquerable man. As so often happens, hunger overcomes the spirit of the strong more swiftly than any assault and forces surrender.

What more can be said? Griffin, compelled by the increasing scourge of hunger, gave himself up to the mercy of the king. Arthur, however, said that he would have no pity for him, unless by the decision of his council. Therefore at the order of King Arthur, the lords convened in court. The decision of these men doomed Griffin to capital punishment. It seemed unjust to all that he should live any longer — he who contrived to commit so great a crime against his brother and his brother's children. And so, after the sentence had been given, God being the avenger of evil, Griffin was decapitated.

Postquam igitur Griffinus (R. p.104) merita exsolvit[1] supplicia, universe primatus Kambrie, rege Arturo annuente, Meriadoci (F. col. 2) cessit dominio. Sed ipse, ut probus[2] iuvenis, maioris honoris apprecians se in florenti etate probitatibus exercere miliciamque expertum ire[3] quam domi residens desidia torpescere, suum socerum Urianum, regem Scocie, convenit, et, quid apud se deliberarat innotescens, omnem Kambrie provinciam eius tu[i]cioni commisit—tali condicione inter se sanctita, ut quamdiu experiunde ipse voluisset vacare milicie, tam diu sub eius tutela regnum Kambrie consisteret, ubi autem in pace reverteretur, ut paterno iure sibi debitum, ad suum, si sibi placeret, rediret imperium. Nondum tamen quam terram peteret deliberacione habita, interim in curia regis Arturi perhendinabat, donec disposuisset, quo ad propositum opus tenderet.

Rex autem Arturus per idem tempus apud urbem liber parumper a bellorum inquietudinibus morabatur. Cui semper evenire solebat, ut, quociens eum aliquamdiu aliquorsum perhendinare contigisset,

---

1   R. persolvit.
2   F. probet.
3   F. iri.

After Griffin had received his just punishment, the first lords of all Cambria gave the kingdom to Meriadoc, with King Arthur's approval. But the prince himself, like an honorable young man, deemed it more worthy to train himself in knightly skills in his youth and go forth to prove himself rather than to reside at home and become sluggish with inactivity. He met with his sister's husband, Urien, King of Scotland, and making known what he was considering, he placed the whole country of Cambria under his protection, with such a condition sworn between them that as long as he wished to be free as a knight, so long would the kingdom of Cambria remain in Urien's care; when, however, he should return in peace, the kingdom would revert to him as due him by hereditary law, if he so wished. However, since he had not yet decided which land to seek out, he remained at the court of King Arthur until he determined where he would pursue his proposed objective.

King Arthur at this time was in residence in the city, free for a while of the stress of war. It usually happened that when he resided for some length of time in the same place, some event of great significance would occur. And in fact such an event did

semper tociens alicuius magni negocii[1] occurrebat eventus. Quod et tunc accidit. Miles enim quidam, Niger Miles de Nigro Saltu dictus, ad eius curiam advenit, Nigrum Saltum suum esse calumpnians, nulliusque nisi sui illum debere subiacere dominio astipulans, quem rex Arturus ut maioris potestatis sibi nitebatur auferre. Econtra rex respondebat predictum Nigrum Saltum sui iuris dumtaxat existere, id sibi assumens in argumentum, quod genitor suus, rex Uterpendragon, duos diversi (F. f. 9r) generis in eodem[2] saltu quondam nigros apros silvestres posuerit, ex quibus omnis grex porcorum qui in illo habebatur processerit. Ad hec Nigri Militis de Nigro Saltu erat responsum, quod, licet minime prefatos nigros apros illius recognosceret, se tamen eorum eo pacto libenter liberam ei concessurum capturam, quo Nigri Saltus possessione et dominio sibi licite uti liceret, "Verumptamen," ait, "O rex, si ex rerum eventu huius controversie consistat probacio, mihi nempe censura iusticie pocius assentire videbitur, qui et ex ipsius Nigri Saltus effectu avita suffundar nigredine et Niger Miles de Nigro Saltu ex ipsius Nigri Saltus mihi nomen dirivetur nomine." Hinc igitur inter

---

1 R. ei *after* negocii.
2 R. nigro *after* eodem.

occur. A certain knight, known as the Black Knight of the Black Forest, arrived at his court claiming the Black Forest to be his property, swearing that it was due him, to be under his dominion and not that of any other man, and that King Arthur was endeavoring to appropriate it in order to display his greater authority.

Against the charge, the king responded that that Black Forest was under his writ as far as this matter was concerned, giving as evidence that his father, King Uther Pendragon, had once stocked two different kinds of black boars in this forest, from which all the swine which ranged there had bred.

To this the response of the Black Knight of the Black Forest was that although he acknowledged in no way the aforesaid black boars to be the king's, nevertheless, with this matter agreed on, he would gladly allow free hunting of them to him, granted that the possession and the authority of the Black Forest be affirmed as lawfully his. He stated, "Nevertheless, O King, if the settlement of the dispute concerning the origin of this matter is brought to judgment, it seems to me that the authority of justice will agree more with me, tinged with ancestral blackness from the effect of this Black Forest; and my name, Black Knight of the Black Forest, derives from the name of the Black Forest." Thus there arose between them unresolved

eos causarum discerpsiones et controversiarum oriuntur litigia. At, ubi discerptantibus finis esse non potuit, isto in calumpnia procaciter instante, rege quoque e diverso illam procacius infirmare nitente, tandem res parium[1] suorum procerum iudicio examinanda committitur, ut quod illi inter regem et suum militem, equitate dictante, decrevissent, dictata equitas utrumque sequi compelleret. Verum Niger Miles de Nigro Saltu, illos quod magis regis gracie cederet quam quod ad suum profectum proveniret decreturos non dubitans, sanius et decencius esse duxit, id quod sui iuris calumpniabatur constare suis viribus disracio(R. p.105)nare quam suspecto aliorum arbitrio committere, dum (F. f. 9, col. 2) ratum et inmutabilie sciebat futurum quicquid[2] iudicii protulisset examen. Ergo coram omni concilio medius prosiliit et "Quia," ait, "O rex, te mihi ex adverso huic cause patrocinari conspicio, istorum me iudicio committere non audeo, quos procul dubio quod tibi pocius quam mihi succedat decreturos agnosco. Unde, quia prejudicium incurrere pertimesco, id quod calumpnior me[3] propriis viribus contra xl^{ta} e tuis quos volueris disracionatum offero, ut scilicet hiis singulis xl diebus unum qui agat duellum adversum me ad

1   F. parum.
2   R. quidquid.
3   R. me *after* viribus.

differences and litigation of the quarrel. When a resolution of the differences was not possible, the knight boldly pressed his grievance, and the king also on his part pressed even more boldly to weaken the accusation. At last the case was committed to the judgment of his lords to be examined for settlement, so that they, acting between the king and his knight, might lessen the dispute and compel each to follow their edict.

In truth, the Black Knight of the Black Forest, not doubting that these men would reach a decision that would tend to favor the king more than it would work to his advantage, decided that it would be wiser and more appropriate for the cause about which he had brought suit to be decided by his own strength rather than committed to the untrustworthy decision of the other men, since he knew that whatever the judges decreed would be fixed and immutable. Therefore he broke into the midst of the council openly, saying, "Because, O King, I perceive that in this case you are the sponsoring opposition against me, I do not dare entrust myself to the decision of these men who I know without doubt will decide more in your favor than in mine. Further, because I fear to incur prejudice in this matter about which I am suing, I propose a judicial duel, my strength against forty of the men of your choice, so that—for example—you will send to the Black Forest each of these men alone

Nigrum Saltum dirigas. Quibus si prevalere[1] potuero, simul et in causa prevaleam; si vero contingat succumbere una et mea causa succumbat." Placuit regi et omnibus quod[2] dixerat, omniumque in hoc convenit assensus non parum admirancium eum adversus tot et tam fortes regis Arturi campigenas[3] solum audere inire conflictum. Erat autem Niger Miles de Nigro Saltu iuvenis quidem sed miles peroptimus qui nullius umquam formidaverat[4] congressum.

Indictum igitur duellum, loco et tempore statuto, iniciatur, ad quod agendum singulis diebus unus[5] a rege Arturo miles dirigitur. Sed omnes, uno omine[6] excepti, omnes a Nigro Milite de Nigro Saltu prostrati, devicti et sub nomine captivi ad eum remissi sunt. Iamque ceteris sinistro fato transcursis, e quadragenario numero tres tantummodo dies restabant, cum rex Arturus, inmodice afflictus, tum pudore, suos validiores (F. f. 9v) equites[7] ab uno devinci, tum eciam

1 prevaluere, *both MSS*.
2 R. que.
3 F. capigenas.
4 F. formidaverit.
5 R. unus *omitted*.
6 F. homine.
7 R. milites.

on forty consecutive days to wage the duel. If I can prevail over them, I will prevail in my suit; if indeed it happens that I should succumb, so will my suit."

What he said pleased the king and all the council, and an agreement was reached, with no small admiration for the man who dared to enter the conflict alone against so many of the brave knights of the king. The Black Knight of the Black Forest was young, but even the best knight fears a duel.

Therefore, the duel was decreed, the time and place set, and it began. To carry it out, each day a single knight was sent off by King Arthur. But all of them, one after the other, were unhorsed by the Black Knight, overcome, taken prisoner, and returned to the king in his name. And now, ill luck having been encountered on the rest of the forty days, only three days remained. King Arthur, considerably upset that his strongest knights should be put down by one man — distressed both from shame and also from the penalty he thought would come of this case — called Sir

dampno quod sibi ea de causa perpendebat oriri, Kaium dapiferum suum advocavit, quem et sic allocutus est: "Intollerabili michi mens merore premitur nullaque per diversa cogitacionum distracta quiete perfruitur, cui nunquam quicquam[1] quam in presenti obrepsit pudibundius. Ecce namque tot mei famosos campigenas quos bello misimus, pro[2] dolor! ab uno subigi, tot viros robustos ab uno pudet enervari, in quorum singulis, quia meam causam[3] agere noscuntur, tociens me vinci confundor, quociens ipsi ab adversario expungnantur. Et de quo celebre hactenus ubique ferebatur, quempiam meorum militum mille aliis prevalere solere, nunc e converso, verso fortune folio,[4] mille eorum non possunt uni[5] resistere. Igitur quia strenuiores mei exercitus hosti inerter[6] loco cesserunt et dies xl^{mus} duobus dumtaxat interpositis instat diebus, vivaci utendum est consilio, ut vel saltem[7] hiis iii diebus nostri simul pudoris et dampni resarciatur cumulus. Unde necesse censui te in crastinum ad initum debere proficisci duellum,

1 R. quidquam.
2 R. proh.
3 R. causam meam.
4 F. filo.
5 F. mille meorum nequeunt hunc resistere.
6 R. inerunt.
7 F. saltim.

Kay the Seneschal to him and spoke to him thus:

"My mind is weighed down by anxiety intolerable to me. I enjoy no peace, nor can I think of anything else. Never was I more ashamed than by what now has surprised me. For, as you know, those renowned, seasoned knights of my personal guard whom I sent to fight have been overcome by one man. So many strong men by one man shamed to helplessness! For my sake they have been assigned to undertake this single combat. I am confounded in defeat as many times as they are conquered by the adversary. And what has happened so far at this celebrated event is carried everywhere: the story that my knights, who are accustomed to prevail against a thousand others, now on the contrary, with the writ of Fortuna having been reversed, a thousand of them are unable to stand up to one man. Therefore, because the more powerful men of my army have yielded from want of prowess to the adversary, and of the forty days, the fortieth approaches, merely two days remaining, it is necessary to use a plan for survival, so that perhaps at least in these three days the past record of shame and loss may be repaired by our men. For this need I have decreed that you set out for the challenge of the duel in the

quem virtute et industria ceteris sepius valenciorem expertus sum et cuius est officium, aliis deficientibus, pro me semper laboris subire dispendium commilitonibusque vexatis et abactis auxilii conferre subsidium. Quod si te eciam victrix manus hostilis eidem quo ceteros involverit discrimini, meus profecto nepos Waluuanius (F. col. 2) contra eum conflictum die sorcietur sequenti. Illum quoque si isdem infortunii casus mer(R. p. 106)serit, ipsemet die extrema ad singulare illius[1] certamen progrediar, quo aut totum cum dedecore perdam seu certe mei esse dominii Nigrum Saltum virtuose decernam. Vade ergo et ut summo sis presto diluculo sedulus previde." Kaius: "Tanta oracionis prolixitate opus non erat tue mentis scire placitum michi; noveris[2] ratum haberi preceptum. Presto ero et rem quo melius potero perficere curabo." Perrexit igitur atque secretius cum amicis secedens, quam lepide, quam generose, quamque viriliter rem gereret cum eis deliberabat.

H oc ubi Meriadocus comperit, qui iam ante triennium ab eodem Kaio ad militarem nobiliter fuerat promotus ordinem, ad eum accessit[3] atque an verum

1   R. eius.
2   F. nolueris, *mark to expunge under* "l."
3   F. adcessit.

morning. I have known you on many occasions to be mightier in strength and cleverness than the others. When others fail, it is you who undertake the effort of hard work for me and, when my personal retinue is pressed and thrown back, you who bring the reserves to their aid. If the victorious right hand of the adversary overwhelms you as it has the others in this judicial battle, it will be my nephew Gawain's lot to do battle with him the following day. And if the same misfortune engulfs him, on the final day, I myself will proceed to single combat with him. Then either I will lose all with shame or else I will settle by prowess my lordship over the Black Forest. Go therefore and see to it that you, completely prepared, are ready at the break of dawn."

Kay replied, "Such a lengthy speech was not needed for me to know what was on your mind. You know that the strategy outlined in advance still holds. I will be ready, and I will take care to the best of my ability to bring this business to an end." He went straight out then, and meeting privately with his colleagues, he considered carefully how gracefully, nobly, and bravely he should wage the duel.

When Meriadoc (who three years before had been knighted for excellence by this same Kay) heard about this, he approached him and asked if what he had

esset quod de eo audierat inquisivit. Quo respondente verum, cepit Meriadocus eum rogare, ut se sui loco duellum cum Nigro Milite de Nigro Saltu sineret committere. Dicens indecens nimis esse et sue glorie minime expedire, ut cum illo confligeret a quo tot probos patebat devictos; quia qui maioris virtutis hactenus ceteris habitus fuerat si et ipse victus sortem incurrisset victorum, maiori nempe quam alii exponeretur obprobrio, quippe dum ad hoc eligebatur ut omnes alios ulcisceretur. De se vero si contigisset devinci, nec sermonem asserebat habendum. Si autem triumphum de tociens triumphante potuisset (F. f. 10r) nancisci,[1] non solum sibimet, sed eciam illi laudis favorem adquireret, quia virtus et probitas militis est honor et gloria principis. Kaius autem ad hec illius iuvente invalitudinem sibique inexpertam causans haberi miliciam,[2] illum respondit qui se sue commisit fidei sui causa tanto nolle destinari periculo, quantum[3] ex bellorum solet provenire[4] eventu vel[5] dispendio. Demum tamen, prefatis atque multis aliis racionibus flexus, ei quod petebat de eius non diffidens virtute concessit, plurimum eum hortatus, ut

1   F. naccisci
2   F. mliciam, *corrected to* miliciam.
3   *Both MSS have* quantus.
4   R. evenire; F. vel *added above line*.
5   R. eventu vel *omitted but* dispendio *glossed* id est eventu.

heard about the affair were true. To this Kay replied that indeed it was true. Meriadoc seized the chance to propose to Kay that he permit him to be matched in his place for the duel with the Black Knight of the Black Forest, saying that it was quite improper and would not increase Kay's renown to do battle with a man known to have laid low so many honorable men. Because if one who had till now been considered of greater prowess than the rest should himself be defeated and incur the fate of the defeated, he would undoubtedly be exposed to greater disgrace than the others: indeed now that he was chosen champion for the duel, he was expected to vindicate all the others. About himself, Meriadoc pointed out that if he should happen to be defeated, there would be no need to explain in so many words. If on the other hand he were able to chance upon victory over the man who had been so often the victor, not only would he gain the favor of praise for himself but also for Kay, because the strength and prowess of a knight are the honor and glory of his lord. Kay replied that since he had committed himself by his word to this cause, he was unwilling to consign him to so great a danger (citing Meriadoc's unsuitable youth and his unproven knighthood) inasmuch as he was accustomed, with luck or with loss, to survive battles. At length, however, he was persuaded by these and many other reasons, not the least being the man's courage, and he agreed. He exhorted him to do his utmost, since he

sic studeret exequi negocium, quatenus[1] non vituperium sed laudis utrique adipisci mererentur bravium.

Meriadocus igitur sub ipso diei crepusculo, armis, ut decebat, instructus, sonipedem ascendit atque ad Nigrum Saltum, moderaciori tamen gressu, ne equus anelus[2] fatisceret, contendit.[3] Ambiebat autem ipsum Nigrum Saltum fluvius latus et profundus, qui, quasi limes et divisio, terram regis Arturi ab ipso saltu dirimebat. Ad quem Meriadocus perveniens equo descendit, faleras deposuit, se in recenti herba parumper refrigerare et spaciari equum volutando permisit. Deinde, crine composito, singulisque membris levi manu comptis et detersis, iterum cornipedem stratum ascendit. Vado autem quo transiturus erat reperto, bucina, sicut alii antea fecerant, (F. f.10r, col. 2) insonuit, quo Niger Miles de Nigro Saltu militem[4] qui secum congrederetur advenisse cognosceret. Niger

---

1   F. quatinus.
2   F. hanelus.
3   F. *here followed the words* amiebat autem ipsum Nigrum saltum moderacrior...contendit, *a confusion of the preceding and following sentences. Scribe corrected* vacat.
4   F. militem *added above line.*

was determined to wage this duel, so that he would deserve no shame but achieve the prize of the praise of all.

Meriadoc, therefore, ready just before the very dawn of that day, having been properly armed, mounted his horse and made his way to the Black Forest, restraining the pace lest, winded, the horse should founder. Around the Black Forest flowed a deep, wide river which formed the border and dividing line between the territory of King Arthur and that land. Coming to this, Meriadoc dismounted, dropped the reins, and allowed the horse to move about freely and refresh itself a little in the new grass. Then when Meriadoc had combed its mane and brushed and cleaned its limbs with a gentle hand, he remounted the calmed horse. When he had determined the ford where he was to cross, he blew a horn, as the others before him had done, the signal to alert the Black Knight of the Black Forest that the knight who was to fight him had arrived.

autem Miles de Nigro Saltu, sonitu percepto bucine, arma statim corripuit, ac, equo ascenso, se curso precipiti ei obvium dedit, quique in medio[1] ipsius vadi transitu ei occurrens cum illo congressus est. At Meriadocus, equum cursu, lanceam inpulsu, caucius dirigens, splendidum ei ferrum sub ore stomachi inflixit, et, cum ipso ictu dextram fortiter impingens[2] ac (R. p. 107) in latus artificiose retorquens ipsum inpulsum prona petere compulit. Moxque lanceam scuto infixam deserens, stricto mucrone, in eum in declivo uno pede scansili retento pendentem irruit; nasumque cassidis leva arripiens quasi ei caput amputaturus institit.[3] Niger vero Miles de Nigro Saltu, supplices ad eum manus protendens, ut secum paucis, pace interposita, colloqui liceret flagitare cepit. Cuius precibus cedens, Meriadocus dextram cohibuit et quid dicere vellet annuit. Qui super equum erectus "Multas cum multis," ait, "congressiones inii, et nunquam me forc[i]orem nec eciam mei parem usque hodie reperire valui. Tui autem impulsus[4] impetu omnis me protinus pristina virtus reliquit, nec alterius modi mihi tua est experta inpulsio, quam si celi et terre una adinvicem, me medio existente, fieret collisio. Dic igitur mihi quis sis, miles eggregie, cui procul dubio

1   F. in medio *repeated and expunged.*
2   F. inpingens.
3   F. quasi...amputaturus added *in margin.*
4   F. in pulsum.

The Black Knight, having heard the blast of the horn, immediately took up arms, and when he was mounted, raced at full gallop to meet Meriadoc, attacking him as he crossed into the middle of the ford. But Meriadoc, spurring his horse, lance couched, aimed precisely. He struck the gleaming weapon below the man's throat, and the blow was parried by the other man mightily with his right arm. He forced that man, reeling, to thrust at him while off balance, turned him aside skillfully; and abandoning the lance, which was stuck into the shield, he drew his sword and rushed the man, now hanging onto the side of his horse, one foot caught in the stirrup. Grabbing the nasal of his helmet with his left hand, he braced as if about to cut off his head. The Black Knight, stretching forth his hands to him in supplication, pleaded for a truce so that he might speak with him briefly. Meriadoc yielded to his request, and holding his right arm back, agreed to listen to what he had to say.

The man, regaining his seat on the horse, said, "I have undertaken many jousts with many men, and I have been powerful enough so that I had found no one stronger, nor even my equal until today. By the force of your attack, all my previous excellence left me immediately; so foreign to me was the experience of your blow, it was as if the collision of heaven and earth occurred, with me in the middle. Tell me therefore who you are, honored sir—you for whom, without

etas (F. f.10v) maturior incomparabilem videtur spondere virtutem, quem eciam nunc inberbem tante fortitudinis comitatur[1] effectus." Meriadocus: "Mei[2] generis originem nunc superfluo duco retexere;[3] pandam quod ad presens spectat negocium, me, militem regis Arturi,[4] hunc Nigrum Saltum[5] contra te disracionatum esse legatum." Cui ille: "Te ipsius militem equidem sum patenter expertus teque Nigrum Saltum adversum me decrevisse prorsus fateor." Gladiumque vagina extrahens ei ab cuspide in signum victorie tradidit. Obsecro tamen," subiunxit, "ut tue propaginis seriem mihi notifices, quia tante fortitudinis tanteque pulcritudinis indolem non reor ex humili plebe descendisse." Tunc Meriadocus, cuncta[6] que pretaxavimus replicans, omnium suorum lineam generacionis natalium, prospera et adversa que pertulerat, sueque mentis ad milicie exercicium propositum, singillatim patefecit. Quibus auditis, "Iuste," ait Niger Miles de Nigro Saltu, "tanto oriundus stemmate,[7] tanta animi virtute, corporisque

1 R. commitatur.
2 R mei autem.
3 R. texere.
4 F. ad hunc; ad *marked for deletion*.
5 F. contra...saltum *added in margin*..
6 F. que *in margin*.
7 R. stemate.

doubt, greater maturity seems to promise incomparable prowess, the result expected when one of such strength is still beardless."

Meriadoc said, "I consider that to trace my lineage at this time is unnecessary; I will reveal what is proper to the case at hand: that I, a knight of King Arthur, am charged to establish title for the Black Forest against you."

He replied to him:"I have clearly been put to the test as a knight by you in every way, and I acknowledge that by opposing you I have lost the Black Forest." Drawing his sword from the sheath and holding it by the blade, he presented it to Meriadoc as a sign of his victory. "I beg of you, now," he added, "that you make known to me your lineage, because such inborn strength and such natural grace I do not think to have been inherited from humble parentage."

Then Meriadoc, unfolding all that we have established, revealed one by one all the forebears of his line of birth, the good and the bad which it carried, and why he had chosen the calling of knighthood. Having heard this, the Black Knight said, "Rightly do you excel, not only from lineage but also for the courage of your spirit and the strength of your body. It

e precellis[1] vigore. Nec me pudet aliis semper invincibilem a tali[2] devinci qualem te iam signis patentibus[3] evidenter comprobavi. Insuper et me quicquid[4] mei est tui ex nunc dicioni submitto,[5] meque, quocumque perrexeris,[6] ad universa que peragere volueris inseperabilem tibi spondeo futurum comitem, quo nec fideliorem nec magis necessarium te[7] reperturum estimo. Pro insipiente reputabitur qui alteri nostrum, altero presente, aliquid mali moliri voluerit." Hec dicens, cervicem ad Meriadoci[8] genua suppliciter flexit seque ipsius imperio (F. f. 10v, col. 2) et dicioni subdidit. Meriadocus autem, quod sibi a tanto viro offerebatur indignum renuere iudicans, ipsius dedicionem cum subieccione gratuito suscepit animo. Deinde invicem amplexi simul ad curiam regis Arturi properabant, accepta ab eo fide, interposita cum securitate fidelitate, ut quoad viveret suo in obsequio fidelis persisteret.

1 F. procellis.
2 F. tale.
3 F. patentibus *added in margin*.
4 R. quidquid.
5 R committo.
6 F. perrexeris *added in margin*.
7 R. necessarium te *added in margin*.
8 F. Merodiaci.

is no shame for me, always invincible against all others, to be conquered by such a one as you have proved yourself so clearly. Moreover, I submit myself now to whatever you command, and I promise that wherever you may wish to go, I will be your inseparable companion. I believe you will find that no one is more loyal or indispensable to you than I will be. For it will be considered folly for anyone to intend any evil against one of us while the other is present."

Saying this, he bowed his neck at Meriadoc's knees in submission and surrendered himself to his rule and authority. Meriadoc, judging it unworthy to refuse what was offered to him by such a man, freely accepted his homage and obedience. The oath was received from him: fealty supported by the solemn promise that so long as the Black Knight lived he would remain faithful in obedience to him. After embracing one another they made haste to the court of King Arthur together.

Omnibus autem xl diebus quibus contra Nigrum Militem de Nigro Saltu duellum agebatur nunquam rex Arturus cibum sumere consueverat, donec qui missus fuerat remeasset. Illo quoque[1] die de Meriadoco quam de aliis magis sollicitus[2] et ipse inpastus remansit et nullum e suis cibari permisit, quousque cognosceret cuius fortune eventus incurrisset. Moram autem Meriadoco diucius nectente, iussit quendam rex Arturus summam arcem ascendere, si quoquam eum repedantem (R. p.108) adverteret. Speculator vero, turri conscensa[3] oculisque contra viam que ad Nigrum Saltum ducebat erectis, "Quendam," exclamavit, "advenientem longius intueor, quem incessus moderacior et splendor armorum Meriadocum testantur. Trilicem[4] enim loricam habebat auream, scutum, interlucentibus gemmis, aureis totum obductum laminis, in cuius equi falleris nil nisi et pallor electri et fulva auri[5] radiabat species. Sed et alium," ait, "a dextra equitem niger[r]imum armis secum adducit, quem, quantum arma et gestus indicant, Nigrum

1   F. Illoque.
2   R. solicitus.
3   F. turi concenssa.
4   *Bruce amended to* tri[p]licem, *but Neil Wright suggests the classical source: Vergil, Aeneid V.260-61, cf. VII.640, "auroque trilicem / Loricam."*
5   *Aeneid VII.279.*

During the forty days in which the duels with the Black Knight of the Black Forest were fought, King Arthur had taken to fasting; when food was delivered he sent it back. On this day, more concerned about Meriadoc than the others, he remained hungry, nor did he allow any of his men to be fed till he learned which man's lot with Fortuna would prevail. Since Meriadoc was longer in returning, King Arthur ordered somebody to climb the highest turret to see if he somehow could catch sight of him coming back. As soon as he had climbed the turret, the lookout stared intently down the road that led toward the Black Forest, and he exclaimed, "I can see someone coming afar off whose measured gait and splendid armor attest to Meriadoc. He has a triple gold-plated coat of mail, a shield with its entire surface covered in gold leaf interspersed with sparkling gems; no less in the trappings of his horse gleam the pale glow of amber and the yellow beauty of the golden bridle. And," he continued, "he leads with him on his right another horseman with black armor whom, as his armor and posture indicate, I predict to be the Black Knight of the Black Forest."

Militem de Nigro Saltu esse prenuncio." (F. f. 11r)

Rex autem hoc pre admiracione credere non potuit, sed[1] et frivolum esse asserens quod annunciabat dicebat tam probum et exercitatum militem ab inberbi adolescente[2] inpossibile fore devinci. Illis autem inde sermocinantibus et diversa proferentibus, Meriadocus cum Nigro Milite de Nigro Saltu, quem manu ducebat, regiam dignus omnibus spectaculo factus subiit. Ac ante regem et eius primates progrediens, "Tuam," ait, "O rex, causam decrevi; Nigrum Saltum, unde causa agebatur, tibi adquisivi; et, si inde teneris dubius, ecce Nigrum Militem de Nigro Saltu, qui illum sui calumpniabatur dominii, propriis tibi viribus subactum adduco. "Nunc ergo premia que victori spopondisti exsolve, ne et ego remuneracionis immunis et tu beneficii videaris ingratus." Huiusmodi enim donum Rex Arturus singulis ad duellum proficiscentibus proposuerat, ut, si quis Nigrum Militem de Nigro Saltu expungnasset, quicquid[3] rediens ab eo peteret, impetraret. Cui rex, "Splendido," respondit, "et

1   R. set.
2   F. adoloscente.
3   R. quidquid.

The King, astonished, would not believe this and said what he was reporting was sheer foolishness, that such a skilled and experienced knight could not have been conquered by a beardless youth. Yet, just as these words and others were being bandied about, Meriadoc, leading the Black Knight of the Black Forest by the hand, entered the royal palace, and the worthy youth became the cynosure of all eyes.

And advancing before the king and his lords, he said, "O King, I have won your case and I have gained for you the Black Forest over which the case was contested, and if you have any doubts, behold the Black Knight of the Black Forest who claimed the land as his estate, whom I bring to you by my prowess. Now, therefore, grant the rewards you have promised the victor, lest I be considered undeserving of your reward and you ungrateful for the service." For King Arthur had promised a boon to each man who fought the duel, so that if anyone should defeat the Black Knight of the Black Forest, in return he would receive a gift of whatever he might desire.

To him the king replied, "You are deemed worthy of a splendid and rich reward. Ask what you wish;

opulento[1] dignus censeris premio; pete quod placuerit, feres procul dubio quicquid[2] nostra sublimitas[3] tua virtute dignum perpenderit." Meriadocus, "Multos tuorum," ait, "huius rei examinacione vexasti que mei est terminata obsequio. Ecce, habes quod optasti, possides quod calumpniabaris, decrevisti unde certabas. Age ergo liberaliter, ut liberalem decet in liberalem (F. col. 2) virum,[4] ut mei gracia Nigri Saltus illi libera restituatur possessio, quam se mei causa desiderasse conqueritur. In hoc enim tota mee summa peticionis consistit, ne suo iure nobilem virum contingat destitui, cuius probitas pocius exigit augeri quam minui." Arturus: "Licet," ait, "pro voto tibi petenda que placeret proposuimus, Nigri Saltus tamen instanciam nos fecisse meminimus; quo excepto, quicquid[5] aliud animo sederit gratanter annuimus. Ridiculo quippe et mentis ascriberetur inconstancie, si tam levis estimem precii, in cuius adquisicione adeo desudavi. Te ergo aliunde remunerari expete, quia Nigro Saltu vestrum neutrum mihi exstat gratum donare." Considentes autem illi ipsius familiares et consiliarii proceres et primi palacii eum hortabantur, ne virum bene de se

1   R. opulenti.
2   R. quidquid.
3   F. sullimitas.
4   R. virum *omitted.*
5   R. quidquid.

beyond any doubt you shall have what our majesty considers to be worthy of your valor."

Meriadoc answered, "You have abused many of your knights by pressing this case which has been closed by me as you ordered. See, you have what you wanted, you possess what you instituted action for, you have brought down what you fought for. Act therefore generously, as befits the generous action for a generous man, so that by your generous gratitude to me, the property of the Black Knight be freely restored to him, which he complains to have been lost because of my intervention. For in this whole matter stands my greatest wish that a noble man not be destroyed by your legal action, a man whose valor needs to grow more powerful rather than less."

Arthur replied, "Granted that we offered as a reward to you the promise of anything you desired, we ourselves have not forgotten the legal process offered us by the Black Knight. With this exception, any other gift that pleases you we gratefully grant. I would be considered foolish and frivolous if I deemed so slight the prize in whose winning you have labored so hard. Seek therefore to be rewarded from another direction, because this request of yours for the Black Forest is not pleasing to me."

meritum promisso et debito casseret premio; quod nec illius probitatem nec ipsiusmet dignitatem decebat, "Et si quod maius est," aiebant, "a te expeteret, annuere de(R. p. 109)bueras, presertim dum hoc exposcit, quod propriis viribus adquisivit. Iustum namque est, ut inde remuneracionis sumat stipendia, in cuius adquisicione laboris est perpessus dispendia." Quorum tandem rex Arturus credens consilio Nigrum Saltum Meriadoc ad quidlibet[1] vellet—datum scilicet vel possessum—iure concessit perpetuo, quem ipse Meriadocus statim in regis presencia Nigro Militi de Nigro Saltu liberum et quietum restituit, salva subieccione et fidelitate, quam Nigrum Militem de Nigro (F. f.11v) Saltu sibi fecisse retulimus.[2]

Duello igitur contra Nigrum Militem de Nigro Saltu pro ipso Nigro Saltu completo, die sequenti[3] Roseus Miles de Roseo Saltu adest, qui haud[4] impari calumpnia in regem invectus Arturum se ab eo conquerebatur avito fundo,[5] Roseo videlicet Saltu, destitui. Super quo dum inter eos vehemens verborum

---

1   Both MSS have quorum libet. (*Bruce's emendation*).
2   F. reculimus.
3   R. sequente.
4   F. haut.
5   F. fundeo.

The royal household of the king himself, his lords of the council, and the princes of the realm urged him not to deprive a man deserving the best from him of a promise and due reward, for it was not fitting for either that man's prowess or his own dignity. "And if that which he asks from you is greater," they said, "you ought to honor it, especially when what he requests is what he acquired with his own strength. For it is just that he receive payment commensurate with what he has earned."

At length King Arthur, trusting the advice of the council, deeded the Black Forest to Meriadoc as his enfeoffment or estate, with all rights granted in perpetuity. Meriadoc himself, in the presence of the King, immediately restored the Black Forest to the Black Knight, free and clear, saving only the oath of fealty and obedience which the Black Knight had made earlier, as we have said.

When the judicial duel with the Black Knight over possession of the Black Forest had been settled, on the next day the Red Knight of the Red Forest came forward, who, having introduced a suit in equity against King Arthur, complained that he had been deprived of his ancestral estate, the Red Forest, by the king. Concerning this case, when a strong verbal plea

accio, racione postposita, nil equitatis censeret, demum Roseus Miles de Roseo Saltu suam causam duelli examini[1] contra quemlibet e regis militibus commisit, Rosei Saltus libera possessione concessa cui provenisset victoria. Mittitur et contra hunc Meriadocus, illius congressum ceteris formidantibus; qui, non minori in istum quam in priorem usus virtute, prostravit, devicit et cepit, sibique socium effectum et sue dicioni deditum ad regem deduxit Arturum. A quo in laboris remuneracionem, ut ipsemet postulaverat, Roseo Saltu Meriadocus donatus et ille quoque Roseo Militi[2] de Roseo Saltu quod ei surripuerat[3] reddidit.

Huic Candidus Miles de Candido Saltu succedit, qui non dispari accione in ius ductus, discerptacionum controversiis sibi non prospere cedentibus, singulare certamen proponit, cum Meriadoco in vado fluminis Candidum Saltum circumfluentis congreditur, a quo et devincitur. Singuli quippe saltus singulis amnibus[4] ambiebantur, in quorum vadorum transitu, semper ab eis est mu(F. col. 2)tua facta congressio. Candidus igitur Miles de Candido Saltu a Meriadoco devictus

---

1   R. axanimi.
2   F. multi.
3   R. surrupuerat.
4   R. ampnibus.

had been made before them, no settlement was reached and nothing of equity recommended. Whereupon the Red Knight of the Red Forest enjoined his case to be tried by a duel against any of the king's knights, the Red Knight conceding free possession of the Red Forest to the one who was victorious. Meriadoc was sent against him, since the others feared to meet him in battle. Meriadoc, excercising no less valor against him than in the previous duel, overpowered, defeated, and captured him; and after the Red Knight had sworn fealty and become his ally, Meriadoc led him to King Arthur. After Meriadoc had been rewarded, as he had requested, with the Red Forest, he restored to the Red Knight the Red Forest, which had been taken from him.

Following this man, the White Knight of the White Forest, forced into a not dissimilar lawsuit with the division of property not favorable to him, proposed a settlement by single combat. He met with Meriadoc in the shallows of the river that surrounds the White Forest and was defeated by him. Each glade was surrounded by its own stream, at whose ford the encounter between the men occurred. So the White Knight was himself defeated by Meriadoc, and like the

ibi, sicut alii, subicitur, in eius societate recipitur et quem amiserat Candidum Saltum iterum, Meriadoco donante, assequitur.

Meriadocus igitur, postquam hos tres sibi confederavit proceres, scilicet Nigrum Militem de Nigro Saltu, Roseum Militem de Roseo Saltu, et Candidum Militem de Candido Saltu, viam quam animo prefixerat ad inquirendam et exercendam miliciam accelerabat. Regni itaque Kambrie, ut pretaxavimus, suo socero Uriano, regi Scotie, tuenda et disponenda negocia commisit, itineris tanti dispendio res necessarias accuravit. Se sociosque, quomodo dicebat, armis, equis et preciosis indumentis instruxit et ad imperatorem Alemannie properare instituit. Missis namque longe lateque nunciis, sciscitatus fuerat quenam terrarum regio bellorum subiaceret[1] legibus, relatumque sibi fuerat inter imperatorem Alemannie[2] et Gundebaldum, regem terre ex qua nemo revertitur, maximas bellorum geri discordias; Gundebaldus quippe, rex terre ex qua nemo revertitur, unicam filiam imperatoris violenter rapuerat nulla(R. p.110)que condicione flecti potuit, ut eam patri suisque redderet

---

1   R. subiacebat.
2   R. alemanie.

others, he became his vassal and was received among his companions; and he who had lost the White Forest received it again as a gift from Meriadoc.

After these three nobles had become his allies—namely the Black Knight, the Red Knight, and the White Knight—Meriadoc turned immediately toward the goal on which he had set his mind, to search out and perform deeds of knighthood. The care and regulation of the affairs of the kingdom of Cambria (as we have said) were commissioned to his brother-in-law, Urien, King of Scotland. He had made provision, sparing no expense, for the essential things for a lengthy journey. For himself and his companions, as he specified, he provided arms, horses, and rich clothing, and he set out with due speed for the Emperor of the Alemanni.

By sending messengers far and wide, he had made inquiry as to what region of the earth was undergoing the judicial ordeal of war, and it had been reported to him that between the Emperor of the Alemanni and Gundebald, King of the Land From Which No One Returns, the greatest turmoil of battles was being waged. For Gundebald, King of the Land From Which No One Returns, had abducted by force the only daughter of the Emperor, and no ransom had been enough to persuade him to return her to her father

natalibus. Hoc seminarium discidii inter eos exstiterat[1] et ad irarum causas gravissimas bellorumque discrimina instimulaverat. Invitabantque et conducebant a remotis terrarum recessibus milites quoscunque (F. f.12r) magne probitatis audierant et crebros excursus mutuasque congressiones omni pene die invicem agebant. Fiebantque utrarumque parcium cedes innumerabiles, desolaciones urbium, rapina rerum familiarum et quod hiis est gravius indiscreta captivorum[2] servitus civium. Inter que probitas et virtus uniuscuiusque in propatulo facile habebatur et quos laudis decere[n]t[3] premia, quosve[4] vituperacionis manere[n]t[5] opprobria, omnium patebat obtutibus. Quibus rebus Meriadocus compertis, cunctis ordinatis et dispositis, illo cum sociis iter arripuit, et, terra marique multis traiectis dispendiis, ad imperatorem sanus et incolumis[6] cum omnibus pervenit. Imperator autem,[7] postquam quis esset et cur ad se venisset[8] audivit, eo quo[9] decuit eum honore suscepit atque inter primos stipendiarios sui exercitus eum constituit.

1   F. existerat.
2   R. capivatorum.
3   *Both MSS have* deceret.
4   R.-ve *omitted*.
5   *Both MSS have* maneret
6   F. incolumus.
7   R. vero.
8   R. advenisset.
9   F. quod.

and family. This cause of strife remained between them and had incited them to encounters of rage and dangerous battles. They had recruited and summoned knights from the far corners of the earth—everyone they had heard to be of greatest prowess; and they waged against each other almost daily assaults and battles. And there had occurred on both sides innumerable massacres, devastation of cities, pillage of household goods, and what is more grave even than these: the indiscriminate enslavement of the captured citizens. During these crises, the prowess and courage of every single man was fully displayed, and before the eyes of all men were revealed those whose exploits justified praise or those whose shameful deeds awaited censure.

Having learned of these things, Meriadoc, with everything in proper place and order, set out for that region with his companions; and across land and sea, transported at great expense, he reached the Emperor with his forces safe and intact. The Emperor, then, after hearing who he was and why he had come there, accepted him with befitting honor and placed him among the first rank of the mercenary knights of his army. Not much later, provided that he would wage single combats and melees continuously against whosoever might challenge him since he was more skilled and more powerful than any of the rest, he was placed by the Emperor in command of all the hired

Non multum post[1] vero, dum ad quelibet certamina singulosque congressus se probius et virtuosius ceteris omnibus iugiter ageret, universis gregariis conducticiis et stipendiariis[2] militibus ab imperatore preficitur; quorum numerus pene usque ad xiii milia recensebatur. Maiores quippe[3] probitates ipse solus cum suis sociis patrabat cotidie quam maxima pars imperialis exercitus; unde non solum apud imperiales sed eciam apud regem Gundebaldum eius nomen celebre ferebatur.

Quadam autem die prepeti cursu anelo[4] equo nuncius ad imperatorem (F. col. 2) venit, referens Saguncium, principem milicie regis Gundebaldi, suam terram cum valida manu intrasse provinciamque[5] quoquoversus depredari.[6] Imperator autem accito[7] confestim Meriadoco iussit cum suis catervis hostibus suum regnum depeculiantibus occurrere predamque quam ceperant de manibus eorum excutere. Meriadocus vero, nil moratus, milites in iiii^{or} turmas

1   F. primo.
2   F. stipendariis.
3   R. quipp.
4   F. hanelo.
5   R. quoque *for* que.
6   F. deprendari, -en- *marked for deletion*.
7   F. acscito.

common troops and professional knights, of whom there were numbered almost 13,000. He himself alone achieved greater exploits with his own companions daily than the greater part of the Imperial army, so that his name was spread in fame not only before the Imperial court, but also before King Gundebald.

On a certain day a messenger, riding fast on a winded horse, came to the Emperor, reporting that Saguntius, the chief knight of King Gundebald, had invaded the land with a strong force and that he was wreaking havoc on every side. The Emperor, having sent for Meriadoc, ordered him and his mounted troops immediately to counterattack the enemy who was ravaging the Empire and to regain the plunder from the attackers. Meriadoc, without delay, formed up his knights into four companies, one of which he retained for himself; the other three he placed under the commands of his three companions.

divisit, quarum unam secum retinuit, tribus autem reliquis suos tres socios prefecit. Fines autem illius provincie quidam fluvius profundo cingebat gurgite, quem hostes prede ducti[1] cupidine vado transierant[2] quemque eciam regredientibus illis traicere erat necesse et loco eodem, quia nusquam alias vadum reperiebatur.[3] Citra huius fluminis ulteriorem ripam[4] Meriadocus Nigrum Militem de Nigro Saltu cum sua turma transmisit, ut, si hostes in revertendo suam manum, fluvio trajecto, evaderent, a Nigro Milite de Nigro Saltu inopini exciperentur. Candido vero Militi de Candido Saltu precepit cum suis,[5] ut adversariis predam eriperet, dum ipsemet cum eisdem congrederetur. Roseum quoque Militem de Roseo Saltu, cui iiii^{tam} partem exercitus (R. p. 111) commiserat, non longe in insidiis constituit esse, qui sibi belligeranti, si opus esset, ferret subsidium. Hoc igitur ordine disposito exercitu, ipse ocius adversarios peciit, quorum itineris et accionis consilium per exploratores totum certius investigaverat. Casu autem evenit quod eis ad predicti fluvii transitum[6] (F. f. 12v) occurrit, maximam predam virorum, mulierum,

1   R. preducti.
2   F. transsierant.
3   R. repperiebatur.
4   R. ripam ulteriorem; F. uteriorem, *corrected above line.*
5   R. sociis *after* suis.
6   F. transsitum.

A certain deep, rushing river marked the boundary of that province. The enemy had crossed at the ford, driven by the desire for plunder, and, now withdrawing, they had to re-cross at the same place, since nowhere else could it be forded. Meriadoc sent the Black Knight with his company to the opposite bank, so that if the enemy, intending to retire his troops, should escape by crossing the river, they would be taken by surprise by the Black Knight. The White Knight with his men he ordered to regain the booty from the enemy, while he himself engaged them in combat. He deployed the Red Knight, to whom he had entrusted the fourth part of the battalion, in a hidden position not far away so as to bring aid if necessary to those of his men who were fighting. The tactics of the battalion thus laid out, he himself at once sought out the enemy, whose whole plan of route and action he had learned with some certainty through spies. It turned out that he caught up with them at that same river crossing, as they were carrying with them an enormous plunder of men, women, sheep, and various

pecudum et diversarum supellectilum[1] secum ducentibus. In eos igitur irruens primo impetu eorum agmen deiecit, quia et preda onusti incedebant et in amnis[2] transitu maxime impediebantur. At tamen Saguncius ad eorum primum congressum universam predam cum sarcinis iussit quam tocius in unum infra agmen coacervari militibusque per cuneos expeditis, strictis gladiis, in se irruentibus resistere. Discriminosum igitur inter eos est bellum conflatum, dum hii totis viribus niterentur que perdiderant excutere, illi econtra viriliter contenderent capta retinere. Meriadocus autem hinc et inde furibundus pererrans[3] armatorum agmina nunc more bellve in hostes irruebat et prosternebat, modo suorum animos variis exhortationibus[4] ad certandum audaciores efficiebat. Ipse quidem virtute Saguncius autem numero militum precellebat. Pungna vero magna protrahitur parte[5] diei, licetque innumerabilis hostium multitudo undique catervatim a Meriadoco pessumdaretur, anceps tamen semper mansit victoria, donec Roseus Miles de Roseo Saltu, qui non eminus infra nemoris abdita pro subsidio latuerat, cum sua cohorte inprovisus a latere in eos excurreret aciesque

1   F. suppellectilum.
2   R. ampnis.
3   F. portans.
4   F. excohartacionibus.
5   R. parte *added in margin*..

household goods. Falling upon them, he broke up the battle order of the vanguard in his initial attack, because not only were they moving forward slowly, burdened with the spoils, but they were greatly hampered by crossing the river. But at the first strike of these men, Saguntius ordered all the plunder and military gear to be piled up in one line in front of them, and the knights, having regained their close formations, swords drawn, faced the attackers. The conflict escalated into a full-scale battle between them; while one side was struggling with all its strength to recapture what they had lost, the others on the other side fought bravely to hold on to their spoils. Meriadoc, like a beast turning in fury from one side to the other, rushed the enemy and scattered the marching formation of the armored men. Merely by shouting encouragement he raised the spirits of his men to greater daring in engaging the enemy. Saguntius himself certainly surpassed in valor many knights.

The great battle in fact continued to be waged through part of the day, and there was no question but a countless number of the enemy were destroyed troop by troop on every side by Meriadoc with his mounted men, but nevertheless victory remained uncertain until the Red Knight of the Red Forest, who with his company as the reserve had remained not far downstream out of sight in the forest, suddenly

confertas[1] dissipare. Turbatis autem et disiectis ordinibus, tunc primum abductam predam pertinacibus calumpniatoribus liberam deserverunt sueque saluti (F. col. 2) fuga consuluerunt. Et quia insequencium ab omni latere telis micantibus via evadendi nusquam patebat, estuosos gurgitis fluctus precipites irruperunt, eo viam querentes, quo nunquam ante viator transierat. Presens tamen[2] discrimen iuvit astucia. Equites quippe super equos amnis[3] medio, quo maior raptus aque ferebatur, magno spacio interiecto, duobus in locis constiterunt,[4] ut rigor aque reliquo transeunti exercitui facilior fieret. Verum idem fluvius nocte preterita aquis nivalibus ex vicinis montibus defluentibus adeo inundaverat, quod eciam ipsi equites egre in eo consisterent. Quia tamen mortis urgebat necessitas, pedites cum equitibus mixtim certatimque se in profundum dederunt, leviorem mortem fluvium quam hostilem gladium sibi illaturum credentes. Submersi sunt itaque fere omnes qui flumen transituri priores ingressi sunt; sed eorum mors ceteris salus fuit. Tot enim tunc undis perierunt, ut ceteri expediti per

1   R. consertas
2   R. tamen *omitted*.
3   R. ampnis.
4   R. constituerunt.

attacked them from the flank and broke up the closely drawn lines.

When their ranks were thrown into confusion and broken up, they abandoned the stolen goods freely to the stubborn challengers and sought safety for themselves in flight. Next, because with arrows flying from all sides a way of escape never presented itself, they pushed headlong into the swirling water, seeking there a ford where no traveler had ever crossed before. Immediately the raging water itself created the crisis. In order that the difficulty of crossing the water might be made easier for the rest of the troops, the mounted knights took up positions in the middle of the river. The greater number of them were swept away, caught by the flood. Great gaps were left in two places. On the previous night the river had become swollen with the melting snow streaming off the mountains not far away. Even the men on horseback stood in it in terror. But because the press of death urged them forward, the footsoldiers intermingled with the horsemen threw themselves struggling into the depths, believing death by drowning less terrible than death by the swords of the enemy. These were drowned, as were almost all who followed in their attempt to cross the river, but their death meant safety for the others: for they so perished in the waves that their bodies formed a ford for those who followed.

eorum corpora[1] transitum haberent[2]. Sed, flumine transito, dum letarentur se discrimen evasisse, in aliud inciderunt. Niger quippe Miles de Nigro Saltu, (R. p.112) qui, ut prediximus, illo a Meriadoco premissus fuerat, illos flumen transgressos excepit, necemque fugientes nece affecit. Meriadocus quoque, ereptam[3] predam Candido militi de Candido Saltu commendans, eos insecutus est extremosque fugiencium exicio dabat. Saguncius autem, ubi suos a fronte et a tergo vidit occumbere, sibi maturius previdens, ad (F. f.13r) quandam annosam silvam que in vicino erat cum paucis elabitur. Cuius fugam cum[4] Meriadocus cognovisset, Nigro Militi de Nigro Saltu[5] totum relinquens exercitum ad delendas vel capiendas reliquias hostium, ipse fugientem Saguncium per opaca silve, tantum cctis expeditis secum assumptis militibus, persequi festinavit, quem mangnopere vivum capere cupiebat.[6] Niger igitur Miles de Nigro Saltu cum Roseo Milite de Roseo Saltu, hostes sine miseracione cedentes, universis aliis interfectis, pene usque ad vi milia captivorum cum multimodis spoliis abducunt atque Candidum Militem de Candido Saltu, qui trans flumen cum excussa preda remanserat, pecierunt.

1   F. expeditum eorum compara.
2   R. habebant.
3   R. exceptam.
4   F. dum.
5   R. et Roseo Militi de Roseu Saltu *after* Saltu.
6   F. cupiebat capere, *marked for transposition.*

But once the river was crossed, while they were still rejoicing that they had escaped one disaster, they met another. The Black Knight, who—as we have said—had been sent ahead by Meriadoc, confronted those who had crossed the river, bringing death to those fleeing death. Meriadoc, leaving retrieval of the booty to the White Knight, followed them and consigned the stragglers of the retreating army to death. Saguntius, however, when he saw his men from the vanguard to the rear guard falling, grasped the situation immediately and disappeared with a few men into the dark forest close at hand. When Meriadoc became aware of his flight, he left to the Black Knight the remaining task of destroying or capturing the enemy, and he with some two hundred lightly equipped knights pursued the fleeing Saguntius through the dense forest, hoping desperately to take him alive. The Black Knight and the Red Knight accepted the unconditional surrender of the surviving enemy forces, taking almost 6000 captives as well as a huge amount of booty. They returned to the White Knight, who had stayed on the other side of the river with the abandoned spoils.

Interea Meriadocus fugientem Saguncium per densitatem silve cum cc^{tis} militibus persequebatur, eum minime comprehensurus. Iam enim a conspectu eius remocius evaserat, atque diende per quandam strictam semitam a via trita declinans, iter quod ad suam ducebat patriam, silva egressus arripuerat. Erat autem eadem silva vasta nimis et horrida, quam cuius esset latitudinis vel longitudinis nullus unquam rimari potuit; videlicet, ob feritatem inmanium belvarum eam inhabitancium et ob innumera et incredibilia fantasmata que per silvam viantes vexabant et deludebant. Tot quippe fastasiarum in ea apparebant species, ut nullus transeuncium ab earum illusionibus immunis effugeret. Quorundam quoque animos, humano sensu, tum terroribus,[1] tum suis transformacio(F. col. 2)nibus, privatos, quasi in extasim ad alia secula raptos dementes effecerant. Meriadocus igitur, predictam silvam ingressus, toto spacio estivi diei post meridiem in eam procedebat. Versperascente vero, in quodam saltu cum suis descendit, atque, equis in recenti herba pabulatum dimissis, membra pausaturus sub divo accubuit, suis vigilibus precipiens, ut statim primo diluculo ad proficiscendum excitarentur. Verum se collocantes, sompnum capturi, vix oculos clauserant, dum ecce aurora albescente, ut sibi pro vero videbatur, diescebat. Vigiles[2] itaque

1 F. terrioribus.
2 F. Vigeles.

Meanwhile Meriadoc pursued the fleeing Saguntius through the dense forest with his two hundred men. They did not apprehend him, for he escaped from their sight, moving farther away and then taking a narrow footpath that avoided the common road and led directly to his own country. This forest was so vast and wild that its length and width had never been measured. Huge fierce beasts inhabited it and uncounted and unbelievable apparitions troubled and confused those who wanted to cross it. In fact every variety of phantasm became visible here in its outward appearance, so that not one of those crossing escaped unscathed from their deception. These phantoms, first by causing unreasoning fear, then by producing hallucinations, drove men one by one out of their senses, snatched as if in a trance to another world.

Meriadoc, who had already entered that forest, continued through it for the whole of a summer's day until afternoon. As evening approached he had descended with his men into a certain valley, and having let the horses loose to graze on the fresh grass, he lay down under the open sky to rest his body, his guard set so that at the first light of dawn they would awaken everyone in order that they might continue on. Indeed, settling themselves down, preparing to sleep, they had scarcely closed their eyes when the eastern sky began to grow light, and it seemed to them that

Meriadocum adierunt, eumque excitantes, "Domine," inquiunt, "surge; iam enim dies lucescit."[1] Ille autem magis sompno gravatus quam alleviatus, valde admirans, excitantibus se dixit, "Vix sompnum cepi, et nunc dies est? Ubi est ergo nox? Certe aut ego prolixiori solito sompno indigeo aut nox solito brevior est." Iussit tamen eadem hora surgere ac[2] iter inceptum carpere. Pergentibus vero (R. p. 113) lux semper clarior sole ascendent apparebat, ita ut, dum necdum miliarium et semis peregissent, ultra primam horam diei esse iudicarent. Circa quod tempus diei in quandam planiciem latissimam pervenerunt, in quam sepe Meriadocus cum imperatore venatum ierat. In ipsa autem plancie subito sibi ingencia edificia apparuerunt, miri et preclari operis columpnis celatis et depictis, celsis laquearibus, ex lapide marmoreo et porphiritico tabulatis parietum constructis et constratis, (F. f. 13v) omnia circumcirca alta fossa valloque prerupto cingente. At Meriadocus ob tantorum edificiorum tam subitam structuram non parum obstupefactus, "Miror," inquit,[3] "O commilitones mei, de tanta rei novitate quam video, unde hee domus marmoree eiusmodique rerum apparatus qui nostris[4] patent oculis adveneriut.[5] Necdum quippe dies xx^{ius} est, ex quo in hac ipsa

1   F. lucessit.
2   F. ad.
3   F. inquid.
4   R. meis.
5   F. advenerit.

day was actually dawning. And so the watchmen went to Meriadoc and, waking him, said, "Lord, get up. It is already daybreak." He, sound asleep rather than dozing, was quite surprised. He replied to the men rousing him, "No sooner do we fall asleep than now it is day? What happened to the night? I must surely need more sleep than usual or else night is shorter than it ought to be." He gave orders to get up immediately and to continue along the road they were following. As they moved out the light became brighter and the sun rose, so that when they had not gone quite a mile and a half they judged it to be past the first hour of the day.

At about this time, they came out upon a certain broad plain where Meriadoc had often gone with the Emperor to hunt. On this very plain, to his astonishment, a great castle of amazing and splendid workmanship could be seen. It was built of marble and porphyry and finished with carved and painted pillars, lofty paneled ceilings, and inlaid flooring—a deep moat and high wall encircling it all.

But Meriadoc, stunned by such an unexpected structure built on such a scale, said, "I am amazed, my comrades, at such a strange new thing which I see. Where has this marble palace come from? How was this thing constructed that lies before our eyes? For less than three weeks ago I hunted on this very plain

planicie[1] cum imperatore et quibusdam e vobis
venatus sum, quo temporis spacio nec tantum opus
perfici nec, si posset perfici, a nobis utique quivisset
celari. Procedamus tamen et cuius sint[2] habitacula vel
a quibus constructe investigemus." Illis igitur
procedentibus, subito ante ianuas palacii pueri pene
xxx apparuerunt, speciosi valde, ciclade purpura et
bisso amicti. Qui omnes venientibus occurrentes[3]
Meriadocum alacri[4] vultu cum sociis salutaverunt
atque ad prandium invitaverunt. Iam autem hora diei
tercia sibi esse videbatur. Meriadocus autem,
quamquam iter inceptum acceleraret, iudicavit tamen
ingredi, hac causa precipua, ut inhabitatores
cognosceret et res tam mirabilis et stupenda sibi[5]
patefieret.

Curiam igitur ingressi sunt[6], quam maxima[7]
multitudinis incognite replebat frequencia, atque ad
hostium aule descenderunt. Inde per porphiriticos
gradus ascendentes ubi regiam subierunt, in
eminenciore domus parte preclarum accubitum
adverterunt sericis pannis nobiliter stratum, in quo

1	F. planicie ipsa.
2	R. sunt.
3	F. occurentis.
4	F. alicri.
5	R. sibi *omitted.*
6	R. ingressus *for* ingressi sunt.
7	F. maxime.

with the Emperor and some of you. At that time no such structure had been built, nor if it had been completed was it at all possible to have hidden it from us. For this reason we shall go forward and find out whose habitation it may be or by whom it was constructed."

While the men were approaching the castle, suddenly outside the gates nearly thirty servants appeared, splendid indeed, clothed in crimson tunics and linen collars. As this group came forward, they met Meriadoc with his companions, greeting them readily and graciously, and they invited them to dine with them. For already it seemed to be the third hour of the day. Meriadoc, then, although he could have picked up the pace and kept the march going, decided to enter, primarily to meet the inhabitants of the castle and to find out for himself the facts about this strange and wondrous affair.

They entered the courtyard, which was filled by a great assembly, an innumerable mass of people, and they passed through the entrance to the castle hall. From here ascending the porphyry stairs they entered the royal chamber. They could see in the most eminent position a splendid couch spread with elegant Chinese silks upon which reclined a lady of graceful bearing

femina decoris inestimabilis recu(F. col. 2)babat, quam et lepidi[1] gestus et incomparabilis pulcritudo nitorque glorie non parve nobilitatis esse affirmabant. Tota quippe domus intrinsecus variis ornamentis erat ornata, nobilesque viri procerum militumque hinc et inde circumsidebant, diversis ludis se spaciantes. Quidam enim simulatam pugnam bifaria acie pirgis componebant. Alii alearum iacturis operam dabant; nonnulli tesseris iactis eventum lucri vel dampni Fortune committebant. Quorum lusum predicta matrona, illorum domina, in accubitu suo iacens, dum contemplaretur, ubi intrantem Meriadocum est intuita, parum se erigens eum lepide prior salutavit et ad se evocavit, omnibus illis[2] iussis assurgere. Ille autem avocatus audacter processit atque super lectum iuxta eam resedit, suis militibus sparsim per aulam assidentibus. Ad quem virago, "Bene," ait, "Meriadoce, ad nos venistis; multum (R. p. 114) enim temporis est, ex quo te desiderabam videre, tuas audiens probitates." Cui ille, "Stupendum est non modice quod video et audio, vel quomodo mei faciem aut nomen cognoveris vel quis in hoc loco tantas structuras tam repente condiderit, cum necdum mensis transiit quod hic nec unus lapis edificii fuerit." Illa ad hec:"Ne mireris, Meriadoce, si te tuo vocaverim[3] nomine, diu quippe est quod mihi et vultu

1 F. lepedi.
2 R. illi.
3 F. vacaverim.

and incomparable beauty. She was sumptuously dressed and, they all agreed, possessed a dignity attesting the renown of no minor nobility. The entire interior of the castle, indeed, was ornately furnished with a variety of decorations, and noblemen and high-born knights attended her on every side, wandering about in various amusements. They had contrived a certain simulated battle with two battle lines on gameboards. Others kept busy throwing dice; a number of men committed to Fortuna the outcome of the toss of the dice, whether it be wealth or ruin.

While still that great lady, mistress of these men, could be observed on the couch, herself throwing the dice of their game, she became aware of the entrance of Meriadoc, and rising a bit, first greeted him graciously and then called him to her, ordering all the others to rise. He, on being summoned, boldly proceeded forward and sat upon the couch next to her as his knights found places throughout the hall. The lady said to him, "It is good, Meriadoc, that you have come to us; indeed for a long time, hearing of your prowess, I have desired to see you." He said to her, "But what I see and hear is quite astounding—how do you know my face and name, or who has built such a structure so quickly in this place where less than a month ago not one stone was laid upon another?" She replied to him, "Do not marvel, Meriadoc, if I have called you by your name. For a long time indeed you

et nomine haberis cognitus. Sed multum erras de hiis edificiis, que tam subito constructa asseris, quia et hec habitacula sunt a priscis temporibus. Nec hic locus est quem (F. f. 14r) tu esse existimas nec umquam nisi modo in hoc loco fuisti. Nunc autem nobiscum comedes, quam diu placuerit penes nos perhendinaturus."[1] Vocatisque ministris, iussit confestim mensam apponi. Qua apposita, solus quidem Meriadocus iuxta illam ad celsiorem mensam recubuit; milites autem eius mixtim cum aliis discubuerunt. Maximus famulatus ministrancium assistebat; splendidus apparatus dapium regalium apponebatur; tot erant fercula, quod numerum excederent, quod sicut postea Meriadocus se astruebat nunquam in aliqua curia vidisse nec tante dulcedinis aliqua degustasse. Verum omnes in communi silencium tenebant, ut nullus in tota aula vel serviencium aut discumbencium cum considente seu conserviente aliquid loqueretur.

Quod Meriadocus advertens, et quia necdum interrogaverat qui essent, circa finem prandii dapiferum ad se vocavit, atque, matrona alias intendente esse curie, quesivit que gens essent, si sua domina virum haberet, nomen quoque eiusdem, necnon et cur ita omnes tacerent, ut eciam cum suis

---

1   F. perhendinaturs.

have been known to me by face and name. Yet you are much mistaken about this palace, which you say was so suddenly built, because this little place has existed from ancient times. Neither is this place where you suppose it to be, nor has it been in this place except as it is. Now then you will eat with us. It pleases us that at last you will be staying here." Having called together her servants, she ordered the meal brought at once.

When it was served, Meriadoc reclined at the high table with her alone. His knights took their places among the others. A great retinue assisted in the serving; splendid utensils were brought out for serving this royal banquet; there were so many dishes that they were beyond counting, so that afterwards Meriadoc swore he had never seen the like in any other court nor had he tasted such delicacies anywhere. But in truth, all the people kept silent together; no one in the entire hall, whether serving or reclining, spoke with the person next to him or to the servant waiting on him.

Meriadoc was indeed aware of this, but since he had not asked who the people were, near the end of the meal he called the seneschal to him, and as the lady had turned her attention elsewhere in the court, he asked who her people were, if her ladyship had a husband, what his name might be, and also why they

militibus qui erant extranei et eorum verbis exhilarari debuissent nullus penitus verbum consereret. Dapifer, autem, dum ad interrogata responsum reddere debuisset, ruga in naso contracta, subsannam ei pro reponso reddidit. At Meriadocus, eum hoc reputans ludendo fecisse, iterum eum ut quesita sibi inti(F. col. 2)maret blande rogavit. Ille vero iterato, more canis estuantis, linguam ab ore usque ad mentum deorsum exerens, subiuncto cachinno, Meriadocum deridebat. Meriadocus autem nec tunc quidem rem ut erat intelligens et derisionem adhuc lusum existimans, "Vir," ait, "eggregie, quid est quod agas?[1] Ego[2] que michi ignota et tibi bene[3] sunt cognita a te quero et tu mihi reponsionis loco contraccionem narium et distorte[4] bucce reddis valgium. Queso ut vel nunc demum interrogata mihi edicas." Verum dapifer, nichil ei locutus, tercio ad instar auricularium aselli[5] ambas manus circa tempora[6] sparsis digitis agitans, ardentibus oculis, patenti oris rictu, Meriadoco, ac si iam eum devoraret, incubuit, vultusque eius adeo immutatus est, ut similior demoni quam homini videretur. Unde

1   F. agis.
2   R. Ego quippe.
3   R. bene *omitted*.
4   F. disorte, *corrected above the line*.
5   R. aselli.
6   F. timpora.

were so silent that even his knights, who were strangers and ought to have been entertained by conversation, were not spoken to by anyone at all.

The seneschal, who should have given an answer, instead wrinkled his nose and in response made a face. But Meriadoc, thinking he was making a joke, asked him again courteously to answer his questions. Once more, panting like dog, sticking out his tongue down to his chin, and snickering, he derided Meriadoc. Meriadoc, however, not yet realizing what he was doing and still thinking the mocking was some kind of game, said, "Honored sir, what are you doing? I myself have asked you what I wanted to know, unknown to me but known to you, and you, rather than answering, make faces, wrinkling your nose and twisting your mouth about. I beg you now to answer my questions." But the seneschal, without saying a word to him, for the third time leaned over him, waving both hands at his temples, fingers spread apart, eyes blazing, mouth hanging open as if he wanted to devour him; with his face thus fixed, he seemed to Meriadoc more like a demon than a man. Meriadoc, no little terrified, sought immediately to rise from the table.

Meriadocus, nimium perterritus, statim e mensa prosilire voluit. Quod matrona advertens, quasi irata, dapiferum increpare cepit, "Tolle, tolle," clamitans, "nec viro nobili iniuriam inferas, ne alicuius rusticitatis nota nostram curiam notare valeat." (R. p. 115) Tantus autem timor Meriadocum omnesque eius socios eadem hora invasit, ut mensa confestim sublata, consurgerent atque tremebundi cum festinacione exirent. Dies[1] autem quantum ad eorum estimacionem, ad vesperum iam[2] vergebatur. Equis igitur ascensis, non plene (F. f. 14v) miliarium perrexerant cum noctis tenebre adeo dense incumbebant, ut nullus ab alio adverti valeret. Isdem[3] quoque stupor atque insania que sibi contigerat eciam eorum equis incubuit; qua incumbente, in tantum debac[c]hati sunt, quod nullus ex eorum sessoribus eorum aliquem domare vel a precipiti refrenare cursu valuisset. Dispersi sunt itaque huc illucque per silvam, quo insania equos ferebat, totaque nocte quasi in congressione pungne, admissis equis, sibi occurrentes; equi cum equis virique cum viris in occursu mutuo collidebantur. Quique dum invicem occurrerent, quisque ad alium clamabat, ut cursum sisteret, manibusque extentis, quisque alium quocumque

---

1   F. Diues, *with "u" marked for deletion*.
2   R. ad vesperium iam *added in margin*.
3   R. Ibidem.

But the lady, noticing, began to rebuke her seneschal as if angry. "Stop it, stop it," she cried out. "Do not injure this noble man, lest he think our court is marked by rudeness." So great a fear came over Meriadoc and all his company simultaneously that, rising at once from the tables, they stood as a body and ran out shaking.

The day, moreover, as far as they could judge, was advancing toward evening. Mounting their horses, they rode but a few miles when the total darkness of night fell upon them, and no one could distinguish one person from another. The same stupor and insanity that touched them also affected their horses. So overpowering was it that the animals became uncontrollable. None of the riders was able either to control any of them or to stop them from bolting. They became scattered through the forest where madness drove the horses on, and all night, almost as if in a battle, the uncontrollable horses ran into one another. Horses with horses and men with men collided in mutual confrontations. They blocked each other until overcome; arms raised, each shouted at his fellow to get out of the way, and each took whatever stand he could and, if he was able, held it against the others. But neither could the horses be reined in nor could they be controlled. Many horses and horsemen with

posset loco ac si se[1] mutuo retenturi[2] arripiebat. Sed nec equi refrenari nec a se potuerunt retineri. Eorum igitur quam plurimi, collisis[3] membris, tam equorum quam equitum sparsim ceciderunt; alii autem per avia ducti a sociis erraverunt; reliqui omnes, una cum Meriadoco in cuiusdam fluminis profundo gurgite circa matutinum tempus inopini devecti, usque ad sellarum[4] carpellas tumescentibus aquis insederunt. Die autem facto, tunc primum quidem ubi essent cognoverunt, fluviumque egressi, licet inmenso labore, quinquaginta iiii e suo numero deesse invenerunt. Meriadocus vero, tantis infortuniis acceptis, magno consternatus est dolore, conversusque ad socios, "O commilitones," inquit, "dies fantasti(F. col. 2)ca nos deliciis pavit. Sed quo fuerimus, quos convivas[5] habuerimus, infortunium quod nos secutum est evidenter edocuit. Tamen ob amissionem sociorum magis doleo, quos scio me minime reperturum."

Flumen igitur egressi parum a labore fessa membra pausaverunt, indeque in silvam progrediebantur,

---

1   F. se *added above line.*
2   F. recenturi.
3   F. colliis,"s" *added above line.*
4   F. cellarum.
5   F. convivias.

their limbs tangled together fell here and there. Others who had been led astray from the company wandered aimlessly through the forest.

The rest, including Meriadoc, at about the first light of morning unexpectedly found themselves seated in the rushing depths of a river up to the bows of their saddles in the rising water. As the day advanced and they began to realize where they were, with great effort they climbed out of the water, and they discovered that fifty-four of their number were missing. Meriadoc, receiving the unfortunate news, was torn with grief and, turning to his friends, said, "Comrades, an otherworldly period of time has overcome us and made sport of us. As a result, wherever we shall be, whoever we will have as companions, it tells us clearly that misfortune will follow us. Nevertheless I grieve more for the loss of my men whom I know I have little chance of finding."

Leaving the river, for a little while they rested themselves, exhausted from their efforts, and from there they rode into the forest, not knowing at all

quorsum irent prorsus ignorantes. Dumque se silvam egressuros sperarent, in interiora eius semper tendebant. Post meridiem aut[em] tempestas valida est eis exorta, scilicet vis venti cum inundacione pluvie et coruscacione fulminum terroribusque tonitruum; quibus malis in tantum quassati sunt, ut felices iudicarent que ea tempestate sub tecto manebant. Anxius igitur[1] nimis Meriadocus et nescius quid faceret, inquirebat a sociis si quem in vicino nossent[2] locum, quo sub aliquo edificio a tanta procella possent confugere. Cui unus militum respondit, castellum permaximum in confinio haberi sed neminem umquam illud intrasse qui sine dedecore exierit.[3] Erat autem inter alios tiro quidam, Waldomerus nomine, cognatus ipsius imperatoris, qui, amore ductus, Meriadocum ad bellum comitatus[4] fuerat. Hic, tam horride tempestatis semper invalescente turbine, dum iam dies vergebatur ad vesperam et iam ictus tonitruum et[5] coruscaciones fulminum ferre ulterius non posset, cepit a milite querere quorsum esset castellum, quod se nosse prope adesse predixerat, et

1 R. ergo.
2 R. noscent.
3 R. exire.
4 F. comitatum.
5 F. et *omitted.*

where they were going. Although they hoped they would be leaving the forest, they were tending always toward the center.

But after noon, a fierce storm came upon them — that is to say, violent wind with sheets of rain, bolts of lightning, and terrifying claps of thunder. They were shaken so badly by all this that they judged blessed those who had shelter in this storm. Very troubled and not knowing what he should do, Meriadoc inquired of his men if they knew of any place where they might escape from such horror under some structure. To this one of the knights replied, "A very large castle is to be found not far from here, but no one who enters it returns without shame."

There was a knight of the Emperor's personal guard among them named Waldomer, brother-in-law to the Emperor himself, who by his own choice had followed Meriadoc to the campaign. As the terrible storm continued to grow in violence and the day was already darkening toward evening, this man was no longer able to bear the rolling thunder and the flashing lightning, and he began to question the knight where the castle was that he had told them was nearby.

ut se (F. f.15r)[1] illo duceret (R. p. 116) rogare. Ad hec miles: "Ego quidem te, si vis,[2] ad castellum ducam.[3] Sed ipse in castellum minime tecum introibo erumptamen predico tibi inde gravissime[4] te periturum, antequam exeas." Cui Waldomerus, "Ne cures," ait, "tantum ad castellum me ducito, quia hic non remanebo." Duxit itaque illum[5] miles ad castellum, quem eciam pene universi qui cum Meriadoco erant, exceptis xi tantum militibus, secuti sunt, dicentes se velle pocius quamlibet experiri fortunam quam sub tanto ibi periclitari discrimine. Miles autem qui[6] illos duxerat, ubi fores oppidi attigit, illis valedicens ad Meriadocum reversus est, qui[7] iam se cum hiis qui secum remanserant sub umbra annose quercus[8] a procella contulerant.

Waldomerus[9] igitur, cum ceteris se commitantibus castellum ingressus, omnes aditus apertos invenit sed neminem in toto castello. Intraverunt autem

1 F. et ut se *repeated.*
2 R. si vis *omitted.*
3 R. simul before ducam.
4 F. ingravissime, inde *omitted.*
5 R. eum.
6 R. qui *added in margin.*
7 F. quia
8 F. quercus se
9 F. Valdomerus, *second* "v" *added in margin.*

The knight replied, "I will take you to the castle if you wish, but I myself will not enter with you under any circumstance. Indeed, I foretell for you that you will be extremely sorry before you leave."

To this Waldomer answered, "Don't worry. Lead me to that castle, for here I will not stay." So the knight led him to the castle, followed by almost all the men who were with Meriadoc, the knights saying that they would rather have Fortuna put them to the test than to risk their lives under such a peril.

The knight who led them, however, came to the edge of the fortress and, saying goodbye to Meriadoc's men, returned to Meriadoc where he was huddled with the men who had remained with him away from the storm under the branches of an aged oak tree.

So Waldomer with the rest of his contingent entered the castle and found all the gates open but no one in the entire place. They came into a hall situated

quandam aulam in superiore turri sitam, auleis co[o]pertam,[1] et tapetis undique stratam, in cuius medio ignis lucidissimus accensus ardebat. Stabula quoque equorum in ulteriori ipsius parte erant, satis habundancia prebenda et foragine. Que cum Waldomerus vidisset, "Descendite," clamavit, "O socii; optime hospitati sumus. Ecce omnia affatim suppetunt quibus maxime indigebamus. Domus est nobis ornata, ignis accensus, iumentis autem sufficiencia pabula in stabulo. Deliravit qui nos ab hoc hospicio (F. col. 2) dehortari contendit." Igitur descendentes equos in stabulis constituerunt, pabula apposuerunt, armisque depositis, focum circumsederunt. Sed dum parumper ibi consedissent, tam ingens timor eos invasit, ut nullus alium alloqui nec eciam intueri auderet, sed, demissis capitibus, terram tacentes aspiciebant, ac si iam sibi necem[2] imminere vererentur. Interea illi qui cum Meriadoco remanserant, ingruentibus noctis tenebris predictaque tempestate semper in peius vergente, ceperunt se invicem conqueri, quod non issent cum sociis sed in tanta procella remansissent. Prefatum[3] militem, qui alios ad castellum duxerat, deprecabantur, ut ipsos quoque ad commilitones quam tocius ducere

1 F. copertam; R. comptam.
2 F. nccem.
3 R. Prefatumque.

in the upper tower, where the walls were covered completely with hangings and carpets were spread everywhere over the floors. In the center of the room a very bright fire burned. There were also stables for the horses beyond the tower, well supplied with fodder and straw.

When Waldomer saw this, he called out, "Dismount, men. We have excellent quarters. See, they are supplying everything we need most. We are splendidly housed, the fire is burning, and ample fodder is in the stable for the horses. A man would be foolish who would try to coax us out of this shelter."

So, dismounting, they stabled their horses and laid out the fodder, and then, removing their armor, they settled themselves about the fire. But when they had been sitting there for a while, such a great fear came upon them that no one dared speak with another or even look at him; instead, heads bowed, they stared silently at the floor as if they feared death to be imminent.

Meanwhile, as the night deepened around those who had remained with Meriadoc and the storm continued to worsen, they began to complain to each other that they were not with their comrades but had remained out in such a storm. They begged the knight who had led the others to the castle to take them to

festinaret. Miles autem, quamquam invitus, dux eis usque ad castellum factus est, sed ipse confestim ad Meriadocum rediit. Advenientibus autem istis, priores a terrore[1] quo tenebantur illorum adventu ad modicum relevati sunt; sed ubi[2] et ipsi cum eis fere dimidia hora consederunt, eodem pavore omnes comprehensi exanguibus similes videbantur. Meriadocus inter hec in silva cum uno milite consistens, tum aeris intemperie urgente, tum veritus ne suis militibus sui in absencia aliquid discriminis contingeret. "Duc me," ait, "ad socios, cum quibus malo si qua sunt participari pericula quam hic sine illis tutus consistere." Cui miles: "Li(R. p. 117)benter[3] te ad illos ducam, sed ego huc redibo." Duce igitur milite, Meriadocus (F. f.15v) oppidum peciit, et, ductore redeunte, aulam subiit. Quem intrantem cum nemo salutasset nec ei assurgeret, "Qua causa," clamavit, "O socii, sic obmutescitis?" Tunc Waldomerus, resumpta audacia,[4] caput[5] erexit atque, "Meriadoce, ne mireris," respondit, "nos ita silere; quia tam immodico pavore tenemur, quod nec nos intueri alterutro nobis mens sit."[6] Ad hec

1   R. timore.
2   F. ubique.
3   R. libenter, *repeated at bottom margin, end of gathering.*
4   F. audita.
5   F. capud.
6   F. fit.

their friends as quickly as possible. The knight, although reluctant, was again made guide to the castle. But he himself again returned immediately to Meriadoc. Once the new men had arrived, the earlier ones, who had been overcome with terror, felt somewhat relieved to see them, yet when the second group had been seated with the others, after as little as a half hour they too seemed similarly seized by terror.

Meanwhile, Meriadoc remained in the forest with only the one knight. Pressed not only by the intemperate weather but also fearing lest some danger might threaten his knights in his absence, Meriadoc said, "Lead me to my friends. I would rather share any dangers with them than to remain here safe without them." To him the knight replied,"I will gladly guide you to them, but I will return here." With the knight leading the way, Meriadoc approached the castle, and as the guide turned back, he entered the hall.

When on entering no one either greeted or challenged him, he exclaimed, "Why, my friends, have you become so silent?"

Then Waldomer, becoming bolder, raised his head and replied,"Meriadoc, don't be surprised that we are so silent, because we are held by such great fear that we cannot look one another in the face."

Meriadocus, "Surgite," ait, "quam tocius; nichil aliud quam inercia[1] vos detinet[2]. Quid veremini? Surgite, discumbite, mensam apponite; nimis enim longa ieiunia continuavimus. Ego autem, si in hac domo habentur, que nobis sunt victui perquiram necessaria." Surgentibus itaque illis et discumbentibus, Meriadocus confestim thalamum unum et alium adiit, sed, in illis nullum reperiens, tercium quoque subiit. In quo puellam mirande forme thoro residentem offendit, ante quam et mensam positam cum pane et vino sufficienti. Meriadocus igitur oblati cibi ductus cupidine iiies utres vino plenos[3] collo sibi et brachiis suspendit, cophinumque placentis refertum inter manus corripiens, ad socios festinus revertebatur, nil prorsus[4] nec eciam salutacionis verba[5] locutus cum virgine. Verum illi properanti quidam procere stature in secundo occurrit thalamo, qui, percuntatus quis esset et cur panem et vinum domini sui furatus fuisset, ex inproviso cum pungno ei tempora[6] eo annisu contudit, ut pene ad pedes eius Meriadocus prosterneretur (F. col.2) gladiusque quem manu tenebat longius propelleretur. Ille autem, de gladio nil

1   F. incia, *corrected above the line*.
2   F. detinent.
3   F. plenas.
4   F. prossus.
5   R. verba salutacionis.
6   F. timpora.

To this Meriadoc answered, "Get up as quickly as you can. Nothing except cowardice stops you. What do you fear? Rise up, get on your feet, set up the table; we have been fasting too long. I, then, will search for the food we need, if there is any here."

While these men were getting to their feet and taking their places at the table, Meriadoc quickly entered first one room and then another, but finding nothing in them, he entered still a third. In this he discovered a lovely maiden sitting on a couch, before whom a table also had been placed with bread and a supply of wine. Meriadoc, driven by his desire for food, hung three full wine-skins from his neck and arms, and snatching up a basket of bread in his hands, he turned quickly to go back to his companions. He left abruptly, not even speaking a word of acknowledgment to the young maiden.

It happened that in his haste he ran into a tall person in the second chamber, who, asking who he might be and why he had stolen the bread and wine from his mistress, struck him suddenly with such a blow of his fist to Meriadoc's temple that Meriadoc was knocked flat almost at his feet and the sword he held in his hand was knocked even farther away. Meriadoc, however, thinking nothing of his sword but

cogitans sed ut que rapuerat perferre posset ad socios, citato gressu ab illo in aulam profugit; quibus et allata apposuit, dicens se quoque ad coquinam iturum. Prius tamen, dum se deliberaret ulcisci de illo qui se percusserat et ensem non invenisset, confusus parum[1] resedit, quid sibi contigisset pre pudore non audens referre sociis. Unde dum tristis resideret, ecce quidam a thalamo venit, ipsius ferens mucronem sibi a puella missum mandante eum rusticum et inertem[2] esse: rusticum, quod se non salutasset et sibi apposita abstulisset; inertem,[3] quod contra inermem ense munitus resistere minime ausas fuisset. Gladium autem[4] Meriadocus adeptus confestim coquinam adiit, lancemque[5] permaximam optimis ferculis que in ea affatim repperit implevit. Iuxta focum autem dormiebat vir inberbis, raso capite, inmanis corporis, qui Meriadoco tumultuante in colligendis epulis excitus, quasi amens, prosiliit, veru quo grues assari solebant ambabus manibus arripuit, Meriadocumque iam exeuntem nactus ei inter scapulas tanta vi veru ingessit, quanta, ut puto, eum exanimem reddidisset, nisi fustis in ictu confracta ictum debilitasset. Ante

1   R. parum *omitted*.
2   F. incem, 'er' *added above line*.
3   F. intem, 'er' *added in margin*.
4   R. vero.
5   F. lanccem.

only that he must carry to his men what he had gathered, fled from him into the hall, where he left the food, saying that he would go to the kitchen next.

A few moments later, however, he began to consider how to avenge himself on the man who had struck him, and, finding his sword missing, he sat down in confusion, not daring to return to his group for shame at what had happened. As he sat there in distress, the same man came from the chamber bearing his very sword, which had been returned to him by the maiden, calling him rude and cowardly: rude because he did not greet the maiden and had stolen the food from her table; and cowardly because, armed with a sword, he had not been able to oppose an unarmed man.

Meriadoc, accepting the sword and finding a lance, went immediately to the kitchen and filled a very large platter with the very best food he could find there. Near the fireplace was sleeping a beardless man with a shaven head and huge body, who, aroused by Meriadoc as he hurriedly collected the food, sprang up as if insane, snatched up with both hands the spit which the cranes held for roasting and hit Meriadoc with it between the shoulder blades as he was leaving with such force that I do believe the blow would have knocked him unconscious if it had not been blunted when the shaft shattered on impact.

hostium vero coquine et penes illud puteus altus erat. Meriadocus igitur percussus lancem[1] concitus deposuit, suum percussorem per aures—quia capillis care(F. f. 16r)bat (R. p. 118) —furibundus corripuit, elevavit, nequicquam renitentem in profundum putei proiecit et cum lance[2] dapifera ad socios profugit. Cum quibus et residens eos alacriter hortabatur comedere.[3] Illis itaque in summa prandentibus, truculentus satelles,[4] gigantee[5] forme, semitrabem dorso gerens, aulam ingressus est. Qui, quoquoversus torva rotans lumina, "Qui sunt," exclamavit, "hii latrones, qui domum domini mei furtim ingressi sunt eiusque cibos more ardalionum diripuerunt et consumpserunt?" Cui cum[6] Meriadocus, socios male tractari ab illo non ferens diucius, evaginato gladio, in eum irruit atque in fugam convertit. Fugientique insistens, tam diu per thalamos, per curiam et per nemus eum insectatus est, donec in sequendo eum in domum quandam[7] armatis plenam circa crepusculum

1   F. lanccem.
2   F. Lancce.
3   F. commedere.
4   R. satilles.
5   F. gigante, *second"e" added above the line..*
6   F. cum *added above the line..*
7   R. quandam domum.

In front of the door of the kitchen and close to it was a deep well. When Meriadoc was struck, angered, he laid down the lance and grabbed his raging assailant by the ears because he had no hair. He lifted him up and threw him, struggling in vain, into the depths of the well, and with his lance he carried the food to his companions. Sitting down with them, he urged them to eat quickly.

While they at last were eating, a savage guard of gigantic build, bearing half a roof-beam on his back, entered the hall. Rolling his fierce eyes around, he shouted, "Who are you? Thieves who have sneaked into the house of my lord and have stolen his food and consumed it like gluttons!"

As Meriadoc tried to answer him, he heaved the raised beam at them, and as it crashed, twenty men fell lifeless. But Meriadoc, no longer enduring for his men to be mistreated by this creature, drew his sword, rushed at him, and forced him to flee. Pursuing the fleeing one, he chased him for a long time through the chambers, through the courtyard, and through the forest. He continued in pursuit until, after sunset, he came unexpectedly upon a stronghold full of armed

inopinus incidit. Dumque armatorum territus multitudine egredi vellet, omnes in eum solum irruentes ipsum remanere coegerunt. Ille autem, dorso applicato parieti, scutum protendit, viriliter restitit, nec ante tum propugnando, tum impugnando destitit, quousque, ex eis quam plurimis occisis, ceteri ipsius pertinacia victi ei dextram darent ac libere quo vellet ire permitterent.

Meriadocus igitur ab illis liberatus ad castellum rediit sed sociorum neminem repperit. Universi enim pre timore (F. col. 2) fugerant sonipedemque eius cum armis secum duxerant. Nescius itaque quid ageret pedester[1] per silvam solus iter carpebat. Iam autem, sole ascendent, dies claruerat; pergenti vero illi fit obvia mulier, veradario[2] residens, sonipedem dextra ducens, lacrimis obducta faciem. Hec a Meriadoco interrogata[3] cur fleret respondet[4] virum suum, strenuum militem, paulo ante a duobus spurcissimis latronibus fraude interfectum, se ab illis captam set tunc a sompno pressis fugisse; quem ducebat velle dare

1   F. pedes, *corrected in margin.*
2   (Veradario, *a place: Bruce's emendation.*)
3   R. interrogata *after* fleret.
4   F. respondit.

men. And filled with terror at the enormous number of men in armor, he tried to escape; then all of them together attacked him standing alone and forced him to stay there. Meriadoc, however, with his back against the wall, used his shield. He resisted bravely, gave up trying to attack, and only defended himself. After many of his assailants were slain, others, overcome by his pertinacity, gave him the right hand allowing him to surrender, and granted him permission to go freely as he desired.

Meriadoc, finally released by them, returned to the castle but found none of his company. All of them, out of fear, had fled, and they had taken away his horse along with his armor. Not knowing what to do, alone on foot he tried to find a way out of the forest. Soon, however, with the sun rising, the day brightened. A woman met him as he was walking along; she was riding a palfrey and leading a charger with her right hand, and her face was covered with tears. When Meriadoc asked this woman why she was crying, she replied that her husband, a powerful knight, had been killed shortly before when two vile thieves had fallen upon them. The thieves had taken her captive, but when they fell asleep, she fled. She planned to give the

sonipedem qui mortem domini sui ulcisceretur.¹ Spondet ulcionem Meriadocus; equum ascendit; cum illa pergit; unum dormientem opprimit; alter excitus et resistens similem casum luit.

Inde digressus, muliere relicta, ut Fortuna favebat, prefatus miles qui in silva illis ad castellum pergentibus remanserat ei occurit. Quem Meriadocus videns valde letatur, ei casus suos² exponit, sociorum turbam amissam refert, se non sapienter egisse, quod ipsius noluerit³ parere consilio. Miles autem ad hec eum consolatus cum eo ultra progreditur. Non longius vero processerant et ecce ante se in quadam planicie armatorum turbam incidere⁴ conspexerunt. Quibus conspectis, Meriadocus iussit militi ibi subsistere, dum ipse ad cuneum quem viderant properaret et qui essent inquireret. Substitit⁵ miles; Meriadocus sonipedem post⁶ eos admisit, extremosque nactus, suos quos (F. f. 16v) perdiderat omnes cognovit una cum Waldomero

1 R. uscisceretur.
2 R. suos casus.
3 F. voluerit.
4 R. incedere.
5 F. subsistit.
6 F. primo, *corrected to* post.

stallion she was leading to whoever would avenge the death of her lord. Meriadoc promised this revenge. He mounted the horse and followed her to the place where she had escaped the thieves. He overpowered one of them while he was still asleep; the other, aroused and resisting, met a similar fate.

The woman stayed behind while Meriadoc rode on. As Fortuna decreed, that knight who had remained in the forest while the others had gone to the castle chanced upon him. Meriadoc was overjoyed to see him; he explained the situation to him and reported that his company of men was missing and that he himself had not acted wisely because he had been unwilling to accept his counsel. The knight, consoling him in this regard, continued on the way with him.

They had not gone far when they saw ranged before them on that plain a company of armored knights. Once he had seen them, Meriadoc ordered the knight to wait there until he could ride quickly to the formation and ask who they were. The knight stayed. Meriadoc urged his horse forward and, catching up with the rear guard, recognized them as all his men whom he had thought lost, even including Waldomer. For by good chance, all of them who, as

esse socios; fortuitu namque universi qui, ut premissum est, ab illo deviarunt[1] paulo ante in ipsa planicie (R. p. 119) sibi invicem occurrerant. Quibus ex insperato visis, ultra quam credi potest Meriadocus exhilaratus est, quia nunquam se eos recuperaturum crediderat. Milites igitur ex invencione ducis et dux ex militum recepcione[2] letificati tractabant mutuo iam fore sibi capiendum consilium, ne ulterius similia discrimina sua incuria incurrerent. Unde adinvicem conferentes, dum fere usque ad tria miliaria processissent, clamor et tumultus pervalidus, quasi bellancium strepitus, eorum auribus eminus insuonuit. Obstupefacti igitur universi se circa ducem fuderent. At Meriadocus, id quoque fantasticum esse existimans, remque prescire antequam ipse illo accederet cupiens, duos equites qui unde tantus clamor esset indagarent premisit. Illi autem interim, equis descensis, eorum reditum[3] in loco expectabant. Nunci[i] itaque festinantes qua tumultuancium voces perceperant iter arripiunt.[4] Sed non longius abierant,[5] cum silva egressi cruentas certancium catervas pre se offenderunt totam quoquoversus[6] terre superficiem

---

1 R. deviaverunt.
2 R. suscepcione.
3 F. redditum.
4 F. aripiunt *corrected above line.*
5 F. ambierant.
6 F. *and* R. quaquoversus.

was said earlier, had wandered away from him had in turn come across one another on that plain a little earlier. Having discovered them unexpectedly was more than Meriadoc could believe possible; he was overjoyed. He had not thought he would ever find them again. The knights, overjoyed on finding their commander, and their commander on regaining his knights, drew up a plan that they would immediately adopt for themselves so that by their carelessness they would not incur a similar disaster later.

Then when they had gone on about three miles, a shouting and a great tumult came from the distance to their ears, seeming almost like the sound of battle. Astounded, they all formed ranks around their leader. But Meriadoc, suspecting that this might be a fantasy also, wanted to know exactly the nature of the situation before he himself would go near it. He sent two knights to investigate the uproar. Meanwhile the others, dismounting, awaited their return. So the scouts, riding swiftly, made their way to a place where they could find out about the wild shouting. They had not gone far when, emerging from the forest, they discovered before them in every direction troops blood-stained from battle. The whole surface of the plain was strewn with the bodies of the slain, with

cadaveribus occisorum stratam, rivulos effusi sanguinis toto campo diffluere. Puerum[1] igitur quendam cominus extra prelium stantem advocant, a quo qui essent ille confligencium turme querunt. Quibus puer: "Exercitus sunt imperatoris et regis (F. col. 2) Gundebaldi." Ad hec ille,"Quis," inquiunt, "ductor est imperialis excercitus?" Puer: "Tres socii Meriadoci[2] exercitui presunt, quos ipse pridie ad hostium spolia reliquerat, dum ipse Meriadocus Saguncium, ducem Gundebaldi, de bello fugientem persequeretur. Verum quia ipse Meriadocus statuto termino ad illos non rediit, cum universo quem regebant exercitu qua[3] eum isse putabant via compendiosiori[4] in eius subsidium illum secuti sunt, verentes ne aliquo tardaretur discrimine. Sed viarum inscii[5] cum inconsultius fines hostium intrassent,[6] a rege Guntranno, fratre Gundebaldi, qui in vicinis regnat, hodie matutino tempore insidiis circumventi sunt. Iamque, ut ipsimet cernere potestis, eorum usque ad internicionem ceditur exercitus, illique iam tanto coartantur periculo, ut in proximo aut morientes occumbent aut certe ducentur captivi. Hostium quippe

1   R. puerum *added in margin.*
2   F. Meriadocii.
3   F. qui *corrected to* qua.
4   F. compendiosri *corrected in margin.*
5   R. nescii.
6   R. intranssent.

streams of blood flowing across the entire field of battle.

They called to a boy standing nearby away from the battle and asked him who was fighting. To this the boy replied, "The armies belong to the Emperor and King Gundebald."

"Who is the general of the Imperial Army?" they asked.

The boy answered, "The three companions of Meriadoc have command of the army, the knights he had left yesterday to see to the enemy's spoils, while Meriadoc himself had pursued Saguntius, Gundebald's commander, who was fleeing the battle. In fact when Meriadoc did not return to the place where they were supposed to meet, they had ordered the army along with all under their command to the place where they thought he might have reached and, fearing that he had been delayed by some attack, they took a short-cut in order to reinforce him. But, unfamiliar with the roads, they crossed over the border of the enemy by mistake and were surrounded by King Guntrannus, the brother of Gundebald, who ruled in that part of the country, and they have been trapped since early this morning. Already, as you can make out for yourselves, the army of these men is being cut down. They are already pressed together in

innumerabiles convenere copie. Verum nec victoribus leta relinquitur victoria. Omnes enim ex adversa parte nisi perpauci qui reliqui sunt iam corruerunt. Quia tres prefati socii, scilicet Niger Miles de Nigro Saltu et Roseus Miles de Roseo Saltu et Candidus Miles de Candido Saltu, tanta virtute in eos debac[c]hati sunt, ut pocius leonum quam hominum illorum videretur esse fortitudo."[1]

Hiis auditis, a puero nuncii conciti ad Meriadocum revertuntur eique audita referunt. Meriadocus autem, sociorum infortunium suum reputans, du(F. f. 17r)centos quos secum habebat equitas duas in turmas divisit, nilque moratus, ad locum certaminis, nunciis precedentibus, quam celer[r]ime properat. Quo ubi ventum est, haud[2] procul tres socios suos ab hostibus circumvallatos iamque capiendos vel interficiendos conspicit. Paucis igitur suos de pristina hortatus virtute, adver(R. p. 120)sarios ab utroque latere viriliter iussit invadere. Nec mora, clamore valido sublato et equis ad cursum concitatis, bifaria acie e silva inopini excurrunt, hostes undique acriter[3] invadunt, invasos dissipant,

---

1   F. fortitu, -do *added above the following line*..
2   F. haut.
3   F. accriter.

such peril that they either fall dying close at hand or else they are surely led away captive. Uncounted numbers of the forces of the enemy are converging. But actually the victory has not yet been bestowed for the joy of the victors. All indeed on the enemy's forward line, except the few who have surrendered, have gone down, because the three companions, the Black Knight, the Red Knight, and the White Knight, have hurled themselves against them with such valor that their courage seems to be more that of lions than men."

When they had heard this, the scouts, stirred by what the boy had told them, returned to Meriadoc and related what they had learned. Meriadoc, comprehending the misfortune of his companions, divided the two hundred knights which he had with him into two formations for attack; without delay he advanced as rapidly as possible to the battlefield with the scouts in the lead. When they had come to the place, he saw not far distant his three companions surrounded by the enemy and about to be either taken prisoner or slain. Meriadoc shouted a few words to his men, reminding them of their earlier valor and ordering them to attack the enemy in force on both flanks. Immediately shouting the battle cry, they spurred their horses to the encounter. The two-pronged battle formation wheeled from the forest in a surprise attack and penetrated the enemy swiftly

dissipatos partim capiunt, partim obtruncant, omnesque in fugam convertunt captamque predam de manibus eorum excutiunt.[1] Adversarii namque eos plures quam erant subsidio venisse putaverunt,[2] ideoque primo eorum impetu statim terga verterunt. Fuerant autem qui capti erant ex imperialibus septingenti[3] quinquaginta equites qui, hostium fuga excussi, eos qui se ceperant statim infestare[4] ceperunt, et qui e bello fugientes se in silvam receperant, hostes abactos videntes, in campum reversi sunt. Occisorum autem ex parte imperialium habebatur numerus cccc^{ti} xxxvi. Ceteri omnes salvi.

Fugientibus igitur adversariis, Meriadocus a tergo cum suis truculentus insistit necemque miserandam ingerit. Omnes enim quos assequi poterant neci dabant. Cesus (F. col. 2) est igitur ab eis universus regis Guntranni exercitus, ut nulle penitus ex eo superessent reliquie. Ipse quoque Guntrannus fugiens a Meriadoco anticipatus occiditur. Per cuius regnum suum ilico duxit exercitum omnia circumcirca ferro et

1   F. excuciunt.
2   R. putaverant.
3   F. septingenti dcc. R. dcc *in margin*.
4   F. & R. infestari.

on both sides. They broke up the formations they penetrated, seized many of the scattered knights, cut down others, and turned the rest to flight. They took into their own hands the captured booty. For the enemy thought that so many men had come to the rescue that they quickly turned their backs at the first attack. Furthermore there were 750 knights from the imperial troops who had been taken prisoner. These men, set free by the flight of the enemy, began at once to attack those who had captured them. There were others who, fleeing from the battle, had retreated into the forest, and when they saw the enemy driven back, they returned to the field of battle. The number of slain on the side of the Empire was held at 436. All the rest were safe.

Now that the enemy was fleeing, Meriadoc grimly pursued the fugitives with his men and inflicted miserable death upon them. Indeed, all whom he was able to reach he slew. So the entire army of King Guntrannus was cut down by them so thoroughly no remnants of them survived. Guntrannus himself, running away, was caught and killed by Meriadoc. He led his triumphant army immediately through this man's kingdom, destroying all the countryside by sword and flame. His forces took control of all the

flamma pessumdans. Potitus[1] est igitur universis municipiis eius et urbibus, quarum quasdam vi expugnavit, quasdam in dedicionem accepit. Prebebat autem larga stipendia suis militibus de hostium spoliis. Inierat autem cum sociis consilium, se minime ad imperatorem rediturum, nisi ante miris a se gestis. Mandavit tamen imperatori bellorum eventus et queque a se gesta fuerant. Imperator vero, illum de singulari collaudans virtute, rescriptsit ei, cun[c]ta que adquisi[v]erat vel adquisiturus foret in sua, prout vellet, potestate mansura. Et, si filiam suam quam rex Gundebaldus rapuerat eripere[2] posset, se eam sibi in matrimonio dotaturum diviciasque et gloriam affatim collaturum. Quibus mandatis ab imperatore Meriadocus acceptis nitendum sibi summo opere iudicabat, ut inceptam probitatem meliori fine concluderet, ne sua inercia[3] perderet quod tanti honoris sibi a tanto offerebatur principe.

Igitur per civitates et castella que ceperat aptis locis dispositis suorum militum presidiis, ipse privatus, usus consilio, tantum cum tribus sociis suis, scilicet Nigro Milite de Nigro Saltu et Roseo Milite de Roseo

1   F. Pocius.
2   F. erripere.
3   F. incia *corrected above line.*

cities and towns of Guntrannus: some he took by force, others he received in surrender. He paid his knights handsomely from the spoils of the enemy. Then he made an agreement with his companions that he would in no way return to the Emperor until he had accomplished a truly remarkable exploit. He sent a message to the Emperor about the outcome of the battles and all that had been done by him. The Emperor, praising him for extraordinary courage, wrote in reply that what he had acquired and would acquire would be his domain. And if Meriadoc were able to rescue his daughter, whom King Gundebald had kidnapped, he would give her to him himself in matrimony, and he would bestow riches and glory in abundance. When Meriadoc had received these messages from the Emperor, Meriadoc decided that he must strive for his own glory with the utmost effort, so that he might bring to a better end the chivalrous exploit he had undertaken, lest he lose by his cowardice these vast honors that were offered him by so great a prince.

Therefore, when he had garrisoned with his knights the strategic places of the cities and castles he had taken, he completed his plans and alone with only his three companions — the Black Knight, the Red Knight,

Saltu (F. f. 17r) et Candido Milite de Candido Saltu, in regnum Gundebaldi regis proficiscitur.[1] Regna quippe horum duorum fratrum collimitabantur, trium dierum interiecto itinere. Iam enim fama virtutem eius usque ad aures filie imperatoris pervenerat. Ipsa quoque clanculo nuncios ad Meriadocum miserat, mandans ei, se ob probitates eius[2] illum solum diligere, ipsius amiciciam[3] oppido appetere;[4] et si ad eam vellet venire, sua industria se e potestate Gundebaldi eripere, insuper et regnum ipsius valeret adquirere. Hoc tamen ei per nuncios sepe inculcavit, ut si ad se veniret, cum manu (R. p. 121) privata accederet, dicens eum potius cautela quam viribus id negocium ad effectum posse perducere.[5] Comparatis itaque vie necessariis, Meriadocus solummodo et tres socii eius iter[6] ineunt. Erraverunt autem in silvam quamdam, quam transgressuri intraverant, biduoque fame affect sunt, quia nulla hominum habitacio in vicino[7] aderat,[8] quibus sibi necessaria emere poterant. Quinto demum die, in extrema hora nemoris, grex boum, quasi de pascius domum revertens, tempore vespertino ante se apparuit. Tunc Meriadocus ait

1 R. proficiscebatur.
2 R. eius *omitted.*
3 F. anunciam.
4 *Bruce suggests words may have been omitted.*
5 R. producere.
6 F. iter *added above line.*
7 F. vicinio.
8 R. e.

and the White Knight—departed for the kingdom of Gundebald. The kingdoms of the two brothers shared a common boundary just a three–days' journey away.

Already the fame of his daring had come to the ear of the Emperor's daughter. She herself, in fact, had secretly sent messengers to Meriadoc, charging him that on account of his prowess she had singled him out and that she sought a pact of friendship unconditionally for herself. And if he would only come to her, with her active cooperation he would be strong enough to free her from the power of Gundebald and, what is more, win his kingdom. It was explained to him by the messengers that if he wanted to reach her, he must consent to come as a private party, explaining that he would be able to see this whole matter through to its completion better by caution than by strength.

Having procured what would be needed for traveling, Meriadoc with only his three companions set out on the journey. But they became lost in a forest which they had entered just to pass through, and in two days they began to be hungry because there was no human habitation close by where they could get the food they needed. Finally on the fifth day in the forest, at the last hour of daylight, a herd of cattle, apparently returning from pasture, came into view.

Nigro Milite de Nigro Saltu: "Festinanter precede; collem qui ante nos eminet ascende; si locus sit quo divertere hac nocte possimus inspice. Hic quippe grex quem conspicimus non longius remota hominum repetunt habitacula." Niger igitur Miles de Nigro [Saltu], ut sibi iubebatur, precessit, montem ascendit, circumspexit, rediit, clamavitque ad socios: (F. col. 2) "Venite; ne moremini; urbs preclarissima muro circumdata trans montem habetur, cuius eciam suburbana firma concludunt menia." Colle itaque traiecto, hominem invenerunt in agro, a quo que et cuius urbs esset urbisque quesierunt aditum. Responsum est ab eo urbem Gundebaldi regis et nobiliorem municioremque tocius regni ipsius esse, ob cuius decorem et firmitatem filiam imperatoris quam ceperat in eam posuisse in eamque clausam observare; portis autem civitatis sedulos[1] continue custodes pre timore imperatoris presidere neminemque ab occasu solis usque ad ipsius ortum die sequenti urbem ingredi vel egredi permittentes.[2] Si, autem urbem voluissent intrare, gregem boum precedentem sequerentur. Intrabat autem grex in suburbana per quandam portam parvulam. Secuti sunt igitur armenta boum, atque suburbana subeuntes ad valvas civitatis pervenerunt repagulis firmissime obseratas.

---

1   R. cedulos.
2   F. permittentes *added in margin*.

Then Meriadoc said to the Black Knight, "Go quickly and climb the hill ahead of us; see if there is a place where we can spend the night. This herd which we can see will be returning to some dwelling not far away."

The Black Knight, as ordered, rode ahead up the mountain, looked about, turned and shouted to his friends, "Come on! Don't delay! A magnificent city surrounded by a wall is on the other side of the mountain. Even its lands outside are enclosed with strong fortifications."

When they crossed through the pass, they came upon a man in a field, and they asked about whose city this was and where it could be entered. He replied that it was the city of King Gundebald and that it was the most important and best fortified of his entire kingdom. Because of its beauty and strength the King had been able to hold here the captured daughter of the Emperor and to guard her in its castle. Diligent porters constantly kept watch at the gates of the city for fear of the Emperor, and no one was permitted to enter or leave from sunset to sunrise. If, indeed, they wanted to enter the city, they would have to follow the herd of cattle moving ahead.

The herd entered the protected environs of the city through a small gate. The men followed the herd of

Meriadocus autem advocans ianitorem rogavit blande, ut sibi ianuas patefaceret. Ille vero tantummodo portarum aperto postico,[1] "Cuiates,"[2] ait, "estis? Pacificene an exploratores?" Cui Meriadocus: "Ex Britonibus originem ducimus; regi Britannie diu militavimus; pacifici sumus; ut regi Gundebaldo serviamus in hanc patriam venimus, quem ab imperatore Alemannie gravari audivimus. Si militibus indiget et nostro servicio, presto habemur ipsius parere imperio. Nos ergo intrare permitte." (F. f.18r) Contra ianitor: "Laudandi quidem estis, quod ad subsidium domini mei venistis, cui talium virorum non parva incumbit necessitas. Verum propter fraudes imperialium sibi assidue insidiancium ab ipso vetitum est, aliquem extraneum hanc ingredi civitatem, nisi ex precepto oris ipsius vel prefecti, quem ad tuendam reliquit civitatem. Rex quippe longius tridie infra suum regnum profectus est, dimisitque in hac urbe filiam imperatoris, quam vi abduxit, ut ipsa eum

---

1   R. posticio.
2   R. Civistes *corrected in margin.*

cattle and, entering the outskirts, continued on to the gates of the city itself, which were bolted with immensely strong bars. Meriadoc, calling out, asked the gatekeeper courteously to open the portals.

That man, opening just a small part of the gates, asked, "Where are you from? Who are you? Ambassadors or spies?"

To which Meriadoc replied, "We trace our origins to Britain; we have been knights in the service of the King of Britain for some time. We come in peace so that we may serve King Gundebald. We have come to this land which we have heard is oppressed by the Emperor of the Alemanni. If the King stands in need of knights and our service, we are ready to follow his orders. So let us in."

To this the gatekeeper answered, "You are certainly to be commended because you have come to the aid of my lord, who has need of such men. In truth, because of the treacherous plots of the Emperor, it is forbidden by the King for any foreigner to enter this city except as he has instructed beforehand by his own words or else by orders of the prefect to whom he has entrusted the care of the city. The King indeed set out more than three days ago from his kingdom, and he left within the city the Emperor's daughter (whom he had abducted by

rogavit, ob cuius ereptionem[1] cotidie pene milites imperatoris per hanc discurrunt prov(R. p. 122)inciam et variante Fortuna plurime hinc inde fiunt congressiones. Qua de re claustra urbis arcius observantur, ne aliqua incuria hosti pateat[2] aditus. Vos autem ite et vobis in suburbano hospicia capite, donec rex redierit vel cum prefecto huius urbis locuti fueritis."[3] Cui Meriadocus, "Immo," ait, "tu ad prefectum vade et renuncia illi quatuor milites ante valvas stare urbisque precari ingressum; simul et cur advenerimus ei insinua." Ad hec ianitor, "non faciam," respondit, "quia non mihi vacat et porte iam sunt claudende. Discedite hinc ad hospicium vestrum; procacia vestra vos aliquas demonstrat machinari insidias." Quo dicto, cum posticum claudere vellet, Meriadocus equo prosiliens, "Obsecro," ait, "amice, tria verba mecum secrecius ad tuum prefectum[4] loquere." Janitore vero negante et posticum claudere festinante, Meriadocus, advertens neminem cum eo infra ianuas adesse, (F. col. 2) pede dextro tam fortiter posticum impulit, ut et ipsum ianitorem postico impulsum solo resupinum prosterneret. Introque fremebundus irrumpens, ipsum per tempora[5]

1 F. repcionem.
2 F. poteat.
3 F. fuerit.
4 F. profectum.
5 F. timpora.

force) as she herself requested him, because the Emperor's knights range through this province almost daily, trying to free her, and they fight frequent engagements here and there at the caprice of Fortuna. Because of this trouble the gates of the city have been very closely guarded lest some careless person allow access to the enemy. But you go and find lodging in the outskirts until the King returns, or else wait for a time when you can speak with the prefect of the city."

To this Meriadoc replied, "All right, you go to the prefect and announce to him that four knights stand before the walls of the city, asking for entry. And also make known to him why we are here."

To him the porter replied, "I will not, because I cannot leave my post, and the gates are already being shut. Leave this area and go to your lodgings. Your impertinence proves you are devising some plot." When he had said this, he began to close the small opening.

Meriadoc, rising up from his horse, said, "I beg you, friend, to let me speak three words secretly with you for your prefect." The gatekeeper shook his head and quickly tried to close the little door. Meriadoc, realizing that no one was with him at the gate, kicked so hard with his right foot against the door that he knocked the gatekeeper flat by the force of the door

cor[r]eptum foras extraxit atque in rapidum flumen, quo urbs ambiebatur, proiecit. Diende introgressus portas aperuit[1] et socios urbem intrare fecit.

Dum hec ab illis geruntur, fortuitu filia imperatoris in turri muris contigua ad superiores fenestrarum absides cum duabus puellis stabat, hinc virorem pratorum, fluenta fluminum, illinc amenitatem se spaciando despectans nemorum. Que, universa que ad valvas urbis acta sunt intuita, statim cepit coniecturare ipsum esse Meriadocum[2] qui tantum facinoris[3] perpetrare ausus fuisset. Verita igitur ne a civibus res gesta comperiretur, sine mora nuncium quem ante ad Meriadocum miserat clanculo accivit,[4] portas urbis adire celerrime precepit, qui essent quos pre illis stare viderat inquisiturum.[5] Nuncius festinavit, valvas peciit, re investigata ad dominam rediit, Meriadocum adesse nunciavit. Remittitur nuncius festinanter, Meriadocum ad castellum perducturus. Mandavit autem illi, ut diceret, mutato nomine, se regi militaturum advenisse. Rex autem, ut predixi, remocius profectus fuerat. Prefectus quoque ad regalia exercenda negocia eadem die urbem exierat. Filia vero imperatoris, ut domina,

1   F. apperuit.
2   F. Meriodocum.
3   F. facionoris.
4   F. ascivit *corrected in margin*
5   R. inquisturo.

swinging back. Rushing in with a yell, he pulled him through the opening by the crown of his head and threw him into the swift river which encircled the city. Then he climbed through and opened the gates to let his friends into the city.

While all this was taking place, by chance the daughter of the Emperor, lodged in the tower of the wall nearby, stood with two ladies-in-waiting at the upper arches of the windows, viewing the pleasant prospect of the green meadows, the flowing river close at hand, and farther off the forests. Aware of everything that had taken place at the city gates, she at once realized that the man who had the audacity to do such a deed must be Meriadoc. Fearing that what he had done would be discovered by the people, without delay she called secretly for the messenger whom she had sent to Meriadoc earlier and instructed him to go quickly to the gates of the city to find out if these were the men whom he had seen before. The messenger went immediately, found the gates, and returned to the lady when he had seen who was there; and he reported that it was Meriadoc who had come. The messenger was sent back at once in order to lead Meriadoc to the castle. Meriadoc had been instructed (as has been said) to come under an assumed name to offer his military service to the King. The King, however, as related before, had gone forth with his military forces a considerable distance away. The

urbi presidebat, cuius iussionibus animo libenciori quam ipsius regis omnes (F. f.18v) cives obsecundabant. Meriadocus igitur, castellum ingressus, filiam imperatoris cum considentibus lepide salutavit. Suumque interrogantibus nomen mentitus, regi subsidio se adventasse cum sociis astruebat. Exceptus est autem ab illa coram aliis, ut extraneus, sed post refeccionem cene, quibusque militum sua hospicia pententibus, puella, cum sui consilii (R. p. 123) consciis remanens, eum introduxit thalamis omnibusque refocillavit deliciis. Cui, cum universa que circa imperatorem et a se gesta erant narrasset, "Mecum," ait illa, "O Meriadoce, hiis duobus perhendinabis diebus; tercio quo te misero proficisceris."[1]

Moratus est igitur apud illam Meriadocus duobus diebus omnique gaudio et delectacione recreatus est. Die autem tercio illucescente, Meriadocum illa advocavit, cui et hec locuta est, "Patens tibi est, Meriadoce, me a rege Gundebaldo vi captam[2] et vi a patre, iam triennum est, abductam. Nec tamen me quasi captivam sed velut[3] filiam, immo eciam ut dominam, semper hactenus habuit. Tocius enim sui regni

---

1 F. proficisiris *corrected.*
2 R. raptam.
3 F. velud.

prefect also had left the city that day to tend to the affairs of the kingdom. The daughter of the Emperor, as the highest-ranking person, was the acting administrator of the city. All the people of the city complied with her orders in both letter and spirit as being more to their liking than those of their King. Meriadoc, then, having entered the castle, greeted the daughter of the Emperor with her attendants gracefully. And when his name was asked, he lied. He further asserted that he had come with his friends to help the King. He was accepted by her, then, in the presence of the others as a stranger; but after the refreshment of dinner and after the other knights had gone to their lodgings, the young lady, with her counselors privy to her plan, led him to a chamber furnished with all comforts. To the Emperor's daughter, along with all who supported the Emperor, he explained why he he had come. "Meriadoc," she replied, "you will remain with me for two days. On the third I shall lay out what you must do."

Meriadoc remained with her then for two days, and he was refreshed with many delights and pleasures. When the third day dawned, she called Meriadoc to her and said to him, "It is well known to you, Meriadoc, that I was kidnapped by King Gundebald by force and carried off by force from my father three years ago. By no means has he treated me like a prisoner but always as a daughter—indeed, till

principatus meis subiacet iussionibus atque ad meum nutum universa eius precipua pendent negocia. Ipsemet rex mee voluntati in omnibus obsequitur, nec est quod velit patrare quod menti mee obesse noverit.[1] Verum licet mihi pro voto suppetant omnia, meam tamen mihi conscienciam semper captivitatis remordet iniuria.[2] Unde (F. col. 2) mihi regnum est pro carcere, diviciarum copias inopiam reputo, honor et gloria mihi videntur dolor et angustia.[3] Nec est aliquid quod meo sedeat animo, quamdiu tenear sub captivitatis vinculo. Nitendum est igitur ut hinc eripiar, quia gratius est mihi eciam cum miseriis mori libera quam cum omnibus deliciis[4] vivere captiva. Ad quod efficiendum neminem te magis scio idoneum, quia qui tot probitatum singulari virtute es[5] assecutus[6] insignia certa sum te meum velle completurum, si ad hoc volenti animo erigaris. Duo autem sunt que huic rei maxime suffragantur. Unum autem est, quod in re militari sollers haberis et strenuus, et, ut puto, solus inventus es, qui Gundebaldi incomparabilem conterat[7] fortitudinem, qui in rebus bellicis nunquam sui parem invenit. Aliud est quod ipse rex Gundebaldus ob morum perversitatem et importabilem

1 F. nolverit *corrected.*
2 R. captivam remordet captivitatis iniuria.
3 augustia, *Bruce's edition.*
4 R. diviciis.
5 F. es *omitted.*
6 F. secutus, as- *added above the line.*
7 R. conteras.

now even as his lady. The sovereignty of all his kingdom lies under my command, and on my approval depend all the significant decisions of this man. As King he yields to my will in all things, nor does he wish to do anything that may be opposite to what he knows to be my intention. Yet, granted that while everything that I could wish for is available to me, the wrong of my captivity disturbs my sense of honor. While the kingdom is for me a prison, I consider the abundance of riches contemptible; honor and glory seem to me grief and anguish. Nothing grieves me more than that I am held bound in captivity. I must struggle therefore to be rescued from this place, because I would rather die a free woman in poverty than to live a captive with all these pleasures. To this end I know of no one more capable than you; the fact that you have attained such prowess by outstanding courage is an indication, I am certain, that you will be able to fulfill my purpose, if you will only stand true to my cause.

"There are two things which are greatly in our favor. One is that you are skilled and quick in military tactics; and as I judge, you alone have been found who may wear down the incomparable strength of Gundebald, who has never found anyone his equal in any challenge of battle. The second is that King Gundebald himself is held in hatred by all the people of his kingdom because of malicious customs and insupportable tyranny; and having heard of your fame,

tirannidem universis sui regni civibus odiosus habetur, tuaque fama audita, tuum adventum ardentibus animis hactenus affectaverunt. Rem autem quo te docuero aggredieris ordine.

Curiam ipsius Gundebaldi a me digressus adibis, quodque sub eius stipendiis militaturus adveneris ei intimabis. Set sunt quedam in quibis te premunitum esse desidero. Ipse Gundebaldus incomparabilis exstat virtutis, cui mos huiusmodi noscitur hactenus fuisse, ut nullum sibi militari[1] (F. f. 19r) cupientem consorcio sue admiserit milicie, antequam quarum esset virium ipsemet singulari congressione fuerit expertus. Est autem ei[2] quedam insula, quindecim ex omni parte patens miliariis, super Rheni fluminis ripas sita, terra de qua nemo revertitur nuncupata;[3] ex cuius vocabulo ipse cognominatus est rex terre de qua nemo (R. p. 124) revertitur. Que quidem insula idcirco[4] terra de qua nemo revertitur dicta cognoscitur, quod sit tota palus perpetua, omni destituta soliditate, que nec hominum nec pecudum umquam tulerit vestigia. Omnis quippe illius superficies insule ad instar bituminis liquescit et

1   F. militare.
2   R. et.
3   F. nuccupata.
4   F. iccirco.

they ardently desire your coming for this cause. You will approach this challenge in the order in which I will now instruct you.

"When you have left me, you will go to the court of Gundebald himself, and you will declare that you have come to ride as his mercenary. But there are certain things about that of which I wish you to be forewarned. Gundebald himself stands incomparable in strength.

"He observes the custom to this day that no one desiring to be in his military service is admitted to the fellowship of his knights before he himself has tested the strength of that man in single combat.

"There is also a certain inaccessible land, fifteen miles on all sides, lying beyond the banks of the Rhine River which is called the "Land From Which No One Returns." From this phrase comes the king's soubriquet, "King of the Land From Which No One Returns." This land is so known because it is totally and perpetually a Stygian waste, utterly devoid of solidity, a muck that bears the footsteps of neither man nor beast; indeed the entire surface of this island softens and flows thickly like tar, nothing firm to stand

defluit[1] mollicie, nulla firmitate subnixa, ut pocius liquidum bitumen quam solidam terram iudices. Inde est — quia quicquid[2] illam ingreditur statim mergitur — terra de qua nemo revertitur merito nuncupatur.[3] Non herbas gignit, non arbores nec aliquid quod vitalem spiret animam. Eiusdem latitudinis cuius et longitudinis est. In medio tamen ipsius, quasi[4] in puncto centri, pene miliarium et semis terra solida[5] est; quem locum, municioni congruum et inexpungnabilem Gundebaldus considerans, mira arte et industria viam permeabilem per mediam paludem ad illum usque direxit. Longissimis enim trabibus centenorum pedum sibique more complium ex adverso incastratis paludi spisso ordine et directo infixis, alios pedis crassitudinem habentes super capita eorum contabulari fecit. Has quoque contabulaciones (F. col. 2) lapidibus stravit,[6] ut natura pocius quam ars viam videatur effecisse. Secat autem insulam a quatuor partibus per medium in modum crucis porrecta,[7] cuius partes coeunt in predictam solidam continentem in medio loco sitam, in qua ipse Gundebaldus aulam venusti operis construxit, [h]ortum diversarum arborum fructuumque[8] conservit

1   F. deffluit.
2   R. quidquid.
3   F. nunccupatur.
4   R. q.
5   R. solida terra.
6   R. stavit.
7   R. porrectam.
8   F. fructuum, -que *added above the line.*

on, so that you would judge it more like softened asphalt than solid ground. No sooner than someone steps upon it but that person is swallowed up, and so it is rightly called the Land From Which No One Returns. No grass grows, no trees, nor anything that breathes the breath of life.

"Its width and length are equal. In the middle of it, almost in the exact center, there is about a mile and half of solid ground. On this place Gundebald, surveying this unassailable area as suitable for a fortress, ordered a road built with great skill and effort to allow access through the middle of the tar pit. Extremely long beams of one hundred feet in length were imbedded in a straight line as a filler or base and driven to the thickened level of the asphalt. He had other logs with broad trunks nailed as flooring to the upper ends of them. This wooden structure was then paved with stones, so that nature rather than art seemed to have made the road. This road cuts the extent of the island into four parts through the middle like a cross. The sections of road meet on the solid ground at the center of the area where Gundebald has built himself a palace of magnificent architecture; he planted a garden with a variety of trees and fruits and

et aquarum rivulos dirivavit. Quam aulam fere semper dum pacis fruitur ocio frequentat, ubi et omnes suos congessit thesauros. A quatuor autem lateribus quatuor castella insulam muniunt, scilicet quibus locis viarum capita ab insula exeunt. Sed predicta semita artissima est, ut obviantes non capiat, trium pedum porrecta in latitudinem. Nam paludis profunditas et inconstancia, laciorem fieri minime passa est. Gundebaldus igitur, ut premonstravi, dum ad se venientes milites et sibi servire cupientes probare desiderat, ipse aulam prescriptam armatus petit, militem ad quodlibet unum ex quatuor castellis statuit; deinde, admissis equis, in arta semita invicem congrediuntur. Verum omnes qui cum eo hactenus conflixerunt[1] ipse prostravit atque in profundam paludem nunquam resurrecturos deiecit. Est quippe vir nulli probitate posterior, habens sonipedem generosum et precipuum, cuius solius valore multos egregios milites ille devicerit et prostraverit.[2] Certus itaque sis te cum illo oportere congredi (R. p. 123) et te ei minime posse resistere, si prefato equo vectus (F. f. 19v) tibi occurrerit, nisi meo muniaris aminiculo.

1   F. confluxerunt.
2   R. et prostraverit..

diverted streams of water here. He maintains the palace as the place where he could always delight in the leisure of peace, a place where also he could secure all his treasure. Four towers on each of the four sides protect the island, that is, those points where the ends of the roadways leave the island. That path is extremely narrow, only three feet wide, so that men attacking cannot use it, for the depth and lack of consistency of the tar pit extends in too broad a band to be crossed in any way.

"When Gundebald wished to test the knights who wanted to enter his service (the custom I described earlier), he would don his armor and go to this palace. He would order the knight to one of the four castles; then mounting his horse, they would meet on the narrow path. Actually, everyone who has fought with him until now he has overcome and thrown into the deep pit from which no one will rise again.

"He is indeed a man of no inferior prowess who also possesses a horse of superior breeding and excellence, by whose singular strength he has defeated and laid prostrate many excellent knights. You may be assured, then, that you must fight with this man, and you will in no way be able to withstand him if he confronts you riding on this horse—unless you are strengthened by my help. I have in my possession a

Habeo namque apud me sonipedem[1] quem Gundebaldus mihi commendavit, fratrem alterius sonipedis quem ipse secum detinet sed illo multo valenciorem et egregiorem. Preclara quoque ipsius arma penes me servantur, que una cum pretaxato equo tibi tradam, quibus munitus ipsius occusum secure poteris recipere.[2] Videas ergo ut te probe strenueque contineas, quia vita et salus utriusque nostrum ex hoc pendet negocio. Si tibi successerit, et mihi succedet;[3] si quid adversi incurreris, et me casus idem manebit."

Hiis dictis, suffusa lacrimis dextrarium e claustris quibus tenebatur fecit produci Arabicum,[4] forma, pulcritudine,[5] et valore sola regia sella dignum. Erat enim capite parvo[6] et macilento, acutis et erectis auribus, collo lato spisso et nervoso, corpore plano et producto, iliis striccioribus, pectore[7] diffuso, crassis clunibus et rotundis, cauda protensa crispa et demissa, tibiis grossis et valentibus, magnis pedibus, firmis ungulis, vivaci gestu, magnarum virium, lenis motus, cursu velocissimus, tante mansuetudinis, ut manu pueri

1 R. sonipepedem.
2 R. excipere.
3 F. succedit.
4 F. arrabicum.
5 F. *Two words in margin marked for insertion here, illegible.*
6 R. parva.
7 R. corpore.

horse that Gundebald has given to me, of the same sire and dam as the other charger which he rides, yet of even greater strength and excellence than his. Also, the splendid arms of the King are housed by me, and I will give them to you along with this horse. Make sure you maintain your skill and strength because the lives and welfare of us both depend on the outcome of our plot. If he submits to you, success will also come to me; if anything adverse happens to you, the same fate awaits me."

Having spoken these words with tears running down her face, she ordered the Arabian horse to be brought before them from the paddock where it was kept — a creature of form, beauty, grace and strength, worthy of the royal equipage and none other. The horse was indeed small of head and graceful, having sharp, erect ears; a wide, thick and sinewy neck; a long back without sway; a spreading barrel; a compact belly; round and firm hindquarters; a flowing and wavy tail; massive forelegs; great pastern joints; and sturdy hooves — a horse with quickness, great strength, grace, and unsurpassed speed in racing, but so gentle it could be controlled by the hand of a boy.

posset circumflecti. Hunc equum falleris quibus condecebat co[m]ptum et ornatum iussit Meriadocum ascendere, supradictis regis armis ei contraditis. Mutuo igitur valedicto, Meriadocus (F. col. 2) ad regem tendere cum sociis cepit. Quem apud unum e quatuor castellis insulam cingentibus reperiens,[1] ea condicione ab eo suscipitur, ut, si singularem illius congressum perferre valuisset, numero ipsius ascriberetur milicie. Quid plura? Dies statuitur, quo invicem congrederentur. Occultabat autem Meriadocus sonipedem usque ad diem congressionis, iuxta preceptum puelle, ne a Gundebaldo comperiretur. Numquam enim Gundebaldus cum eo certamen inisset, si illum equum Meriadocum habere cognovisset. Duelli dies advenerat et uterque se ad certamen preparat. Rex ab aula in insula sita, Meriadocus a proximo castello armatus progreditur. Verum ubi appropinquaverunt et rex Gundebaldus suum sonipedem advertit, confestim expaluit, omneque robur ipsius emarcuit; in sortibus quippe acceperat se ab illo solo vincendum qui sibi singulari pungna illo equo vectus occurrisset. Non tamen erat tunc tempus penitendi nec locus periculum evitandi, quia, ut alter libere transiret, alterum[2] deici ante erat necesse. Tota igitur res solis consistebat viribus. Hec tamen[3] horrenda voce intonuit, se ab illis proditum

1   F. repperiens.
2   F. alter.
3   R. tantum.

When the horse had been harnessed and outfitted with the elaborate trappings that were customary, she ordered Meriadoc, who had been armed with the royal armor she had given to him, to mount. After they bade one another farewell, he began the journey to the King, accompanied by his companions.

Once they had found Gundebald in one of the four castles encircling the island, Meriadoc was received by him on the condition that if he proved to be the stronger in single combat with him, he would then enroll him in the number of his knights.

What more? The day on which they would meet one another was set. Meriadoc, however, hid the charger until the day of the duel, following the instructions of the maiden, lest Gundebald find out. Gundebald, to be sure, did not know whom he was to challenge, but he would have known had he seen Meriadoc with the horse.

The day of the duel came, and each prepared himself for combat. From the palace on the island the King came forth fully armed, and Meriadoc from the nearby tower. Then when they drew nearer and King Gundebald recognized his own steed, he paled immediately and all his oak-like strength withered in him. In fact, he had learned through casting lots that he could be conquered only by the man who would

inquibus maxime confidebat, subiu[n]xitque, "Meriadoce, Meriadoce, nunc primum quis sis agnosco, tua cum puella amicicia supplantavit (R. p.126) me." Meriadocus autem eius dicta non attendens, a[d]misso equo, demissa lancea, eum viriliter impulit, atque cum equo (F. f. 20r) in unum globum, versis vestigiis, in paludem deiecit. Absor[p]tique sunt ambo, scilicet rex cum sonipede, in profundo bituminis nec unquam postea visi sunt.

Rege igitur Gundebaldo in palude submerso, quia propter vie artitudinem equum Meriadocus circumflectere minime poterat, usque ad aulam progressus est. Ex cuius adventu milites, custodes palacii, regis interitum cognoscentes, sine mora in ultionem domini[1] in eum unanimes irruissent, ni pacta condicio et lex statuta vetuissent. Sanctitum namque inter regem et Meriadocum iureiurando, suo universo audiente exercitu, fuerat, ut, si, illo devicto, Meriadocus

---

1   F. ultiorem dum.

meet him in single combat mounted on that horse. Nevertheless it was not the time for regrets nor the place for evading danger, because if one man were to cross freely, it would be necessary for the other to be thrown down. The entire issue rested on strength. He screamed in a horrible voice that he had been betrayed by those on whom he relied the most and shouted, "Meriadoc, Meriadoc, now at last I know who you are. Your pact with the maiden has overthrown me."

Meriadoc, however, paying no attention to these words, urged his horse forward, lowered his lance, struck him violently, and, reversing his horse, cast him with his horse together as one into the pit. They went down together, the King with his horse, into the depths of the tar and were never seen again.

When King Gundebald had disappeared into the morass, Meriadoc was able with no little skill to turn his horse about on the narrow path and ride toward the palace. At his coming, the knights who were the palace guards, realizing the King had been slain, would have attacked him immediately with one accord in vengeance for their lord, except that the conditions of the pact and the established law forbade it. Thereupon the sanctity of the oath between the King and Meriadoc, made in the hearing of his entire army, remained: that if the King were conquered, Meriadoc

victor existeret,[1] ob ipsius necem nil prorsus[2] mali a
suorum quoquam pateretur. Et, quia herede carebat,
suo quoque libere potiretur imperio. Tot quippe ante[3]
Meriadocum secum confligentes prostraverat, ut nec
ipsum quidem sibi posse resistere certus extiterit.
Ideoque pactum huiusmodi quasi pro ridiculo cum eo
inierit. Sed longe aliter quam sperabatur contigit.
Aulici igitur, tum condicione sanctita constricti, tum
eius probitatem admirati, non solum ei nocere
caverunt, verum eciam cum ingenti ipsum laude
susceperunt, ut dominum acclamantes[4] illum dignum
imperio, qui virum contriverit, cuius impetum
neminem umquam ferre potuisse constabat. Arma
itaque thesaurosque ei contradunt. Mittit confestim
pro sociis ad castellum de quo ad bellum egressus est.
Nunciatur quoque (F. col. 2) res gesta per reliqua
oppida confinia. Conveniunt ad Meriadocum
principes; coadunantur militum cohortes; in regni
gubernatorem ab omnibus assumitur, summaque
rerum potestas ei conceditur. Deditur illi universa
provincia; tocius regni cessit potencia. Meriadocus
autem, eorum liberalitati et munificencie debitas
gracias referens condignisque muneribus singulos

1 F. exissteret.
2 F. prosus.
3 F. autem.
4 R. acclammantes.

would stand as the victor on account of the death of that man, barring no treachery by Meriadoc's men being witnessed by anyone. Not only that, but since the King had no heir, Meriadoc might assume posession of the realm without restriction. So many men had fallen fighting against Meriadoc and his men that it was certain that no one of the King's men would be able to resist him. Actually Gundebald had entered a pact of this sort with Meriadoc almost as a joke. But the outcome was far different from what he had expected. The courtiers then, constrained by the sworn contract and also impressed by Meriadoc's prowess – not merely concerned about injury from him, but in truth also admiring him greatly – received him with praise, acclaiming him worthy to be lord of the realm, the one who had destroyed the man whose force no one before had been able to withstand. And so they surrendered to him their arms and treasure. He at once sent for his comrades at the tower from which he had gone forth for the duel.

The news was announced through the remaining castles of the kingdom. The lords then came to Meriadoc, and the ranks of knights were assembled; he was accepted by all as the ruler of the kingdom and the highest authority in governmental decisions was ceded to him. The entire country gave him homage; the military might of the entire kingdom yielded to him. Meriadoc, then, giving thanks for their

remunerans, illis in commune insinuat, quod miles sit imperatoris; quod ab eo ad subiugandos hostes directus; quod hiis rebus maxime suam operam adhibuerit, ut filiam imperatoris a captivate excuteret; quod quicquid[1] illis in regionibus adquisisset viribus et nomini imperatoris ascriberet; quod imperator[2] sibi filiam se in matrimonio daturum, si eam e Gundebaldi posset manibus eripere, spoponderit; propter que omnia oportere se consensu, consilio et ordinacione imperatoris agere, que agenda erant super regnorum que[3] assecutus fuerat regimine. Ad hec principes ex communi responderunt consultu, se nichil imperatori debere; se nichil ex ipso tenere; se nunquam sub eius dicione fuisse; se nec timore nec viribus imperatoris sibi cessisse. Si traditum a se principatum in antiqua libertate vellet tueri, gratum ilius sibi foret dominium; si sub imperatoris deli(R. p. 127)beraret transferre[4] imperium, iret quo vellet, ut venerat; ipsi sibi alium regem preficerent. Dum hoc inter eos diu ventilatum fuisset, tandem in (F. f. 10v) hac se[n]tencia consenserunt principes, ut, si imperator ei suam filiam in coniugium traderet, regnum suum imperatoris dicioni subigi non refutarent. Sin autem, id nullo

1 R. quidquid.
2 R. imperatorem.
3 R. quo.
4 R. sub imperatore deliverare tran[s]ferret.

generosity and munificence and rewarding each one with worthy gifts, explained to them all assembled that because he was the knight of the Emperor, because he had been ordered by him to conquer the enemy, because he had undertaken the task especially so that he might reclaim the daughter of the Emperor from captivity, because whatever he had acquired in those regions he ascribed to the power and name of the Emperor, because the Emperor had promised to give his daughter to him in matrimony if he could rescue her from the hands of Gundebald — therefore he not only had followed strictly everything agreed upon by him, but following the plan and strategy of the Emperor, he had promised that these also would be followed in regard to the royal authority of the kingdoms.

To all this the lords responded from their common council that he owed nothing to the Emperor, that he held nothing of him, that he was not under fealty to him, that he should not submit himself out of fear nor because of the forces of the Emperor. If he wished to claim for himself the surrendered sovereignty in its ancient freedom, the lordship of this land would be given to him. However, if he was determined to transfer the sovereignty to the Emperor, it would go as he wished, as he held dominion. They themselves would placed him in authority as if he were the king. When this matter had been aired among them at

modo fieri paterentur. Tali fine conventus solvitur. Meriadocus autem, munitis undecumque urbibus et castellis, ad puellam rediit, a qua cum magna triumphali pompa magnisque[1] occurrencium est exceptus preconiis.

Dum autem Meriadocus in hiis esset occupatus negociis, ingens bellum inter imperatorem et regem Gallie exoritur, quo imperatorem valde comprimi et coartari contigit. Rex quippe Gallie ex inproviso super eum ducens exercitum, longe lateque eius depeculiatus provincias, quasdam quoque preclaras urbes et municipia expugnavit, cives captivavit, reliqua omnia ferro et flamma pessumdans. Tres eciam ipsius duces cum maxima multitudine sibi occurrentes prostravit omnemque eorum usque ad internicionem fudit[2] exercitum. Imminente igitur sibi rege et assidua infestacione incumbente, compulsus est imperator cum eo pacem firmare talique[3] condicione inire concordiam, ut filiam suam quam Gundebaldo Meriadocus

---

1   F. mangnisque.
2   R. fudit *added in margin.*
3   F. -que *omitted.*

length, the lords concurred in the decision that, if the Emperor gave Meriadoc his daughter in marriage, they would not deny the giving of fealty for their kingdom to the Emperor. If the Emperor did not, however, this agreement would be null and void. Thus at last the issue was resolved. Meriadoc, then, having seen to the defenses of the towns and castles, returned to the maiden, by whom he was received with a triumphal procession and magnificent ceremony.

However, while Meriadoc was occupied in these affairs of state, bitter war arose between the Emperor and the King of Gaul, who was pressing the forces of the Emperor and driving them back. The King of Gaul, leading his army against him in a surprise move, had pillaged the length and breadth of his provinces, raided some of his most splendid cities and castles, taking the people captive and razing the countryside by sword and fire. He had conquered three of the Emperor's dukes who had mounted a counter-attack with a great number of men, and he routed the entire army almost to destruction. With the unremitting and continuously hostile attacks falling upon him, the Emperor was forced to negotiate peace with the King, and the conditions to initiate a concord were such that he would unite his daughter (the young woman Meriadoc had rescued from Gundebald) with the King

eripuerat maritali lege coniungeret, concessis ei omnibus que de suo imperio armis optinuerat. Iam quippe ei Meriadocus universa a se gesta scripto innotuerat. Cavit autem diligentissime imperator ne quod (F. col. 2) cum rege Gallie super filie sue desponsacione convenerat, ullo modo Meriadoco patefieret; unde et ad huius rei noticiam non nisi consiliarios suos quemquam admiserat. Noverat enim probitatem Meriadoci et quantum in re militari valeret quantumque iam sibi ex duobus regnis que adquisi[v]erat robur accrevisset. Studuit itaque eum fraude circumvenire, qua filiam suam de manibus eius auferre ipsumque sui potestati posset subigere.

Hec imperator apud se et cum amicis deliberans, duos nobilissimos proceres, xl suo in comitatu[1] milites habentes, ad Meriadocum cum suis signatis direxit apicibus, quibus primum Meriadocum laude efferebat[2] multiplici, illum patronum et tutorem sui sepe clamitans imperii. Deinde dignas laboribus ipsius remuneraciones promittebat; quedam quoque de propriis[3] negociis que circa se versabantur interserebat.[4] Ad ultimum vero mandabat et precipiebat

1 F. commitatu.
2 F. afferebat.
3 F. propriiis.
4 F. interserabat.

he had taken from the Empire by force of arms. This was done even though Meriadoc had made known to him in writing everything that he had accomplished. For this reason the Emperor was extremely careful lest what he had agreed concerning his daughter's betrothal to the King of Gaul be revealed to Meriadoc in any way; he further allowed no notice at all of this treaty to be sent to any of his counselors. For he knew the prowess of Meriadoc and the extent of his brilliance in military strategy, and how much already his authority had grown as a result of the two kingdoms he had won for him. The Emperor undertook therefore to trap him by treachery so that he could regain his daughter from his hands and be able to subdue the man himself to his own power.

The Emperor kept this to himself, and with his council he made plans to send two of his most noble courtiers, with an escort of forty knights of his own household, to Meriadoc with a message under his own seal by which he first gave Meriadoc much praise, proclaiming him lord and regent of the Empire many times. He then promised rewards worthy of the efforts of the man himself; he hinted at what everyone was saying about Meriadoc concerning his personal achievements. In conclusion, he ordered Meriadoc to

illum sine dilacione ad se properare, suam filiam cum principibus utriusque regni adducere, tum quia eam visendi nimio detinebatur affectu, tum quod nupcias eiusdem peragere festinaret, quas se absente perfici nolebat, tum eciam ut[1] principes quos convenire iubebat sibi dedicionem facerent. Meriadocus, autem, huiusmodi ab imperatore mandata suscipiens, magnum sue glorie ex dictis ipsius repu(F. f. 21r)tabat emolumentum accidisse, non perpendens hamum cibo tectum, venenum melle dulcoratum, verba captancia decepcionis blandiciis illita extitisse. Nec mora, procerum coegit concilium in quorum audiencia mandata imperatoris recitari iussit. (R. p.128) Quibus auditis, confestim favor cunctorum eum assecutus est, illum dignum acclamantium[2] regni gubernacione qui tot et tanta a tanto principe percipere meruisset laudum preconia. Promiseruntque se cum illo una ituros eique in omnibus que imperasset obsecundaturos et quicumque casus manerent socios fore atque participes.

Cum maximo igitur[3] decore atque nobilitate profeccione parata, Meriadocus, assumpta filia imperatoris, iter propositum arrip[u]it. Comitabantur[4]

1   F. ut *omitted.*
2   F. acclammancium.
3   F. igitur *added above line.*
4   F. commitabantur.

come to him and instructed him to bring his daughter along with the lords and the other prominent men of the kingdom, not only because he desired to see her so greatly, but also because he could hasten to arrange their nuptials, which he was unwilling to have performed in his absence, and further so that the lords whom he ordered to assemble could make their official surrender to him.

Meriadoc, receiving a mandate like this from the Emperor, assumed that great benefits would accrue as recognition of his exploits as the Emperor had promised, not realizing that the bait hides the hook, that honey sweetens poison, or that deceptive flattery can smear crafty words. Without delay he gathered together the lords in council in whose hearing he ordered the mandate of the Emperor read. When they had heard it, the approval of the entire assembly was granted him immediately. They affirmed with cheers that he was worthy of the rule of the kingdom, he who had earned so great a number of declarations of praise by so eminent a prince; and they promised they would accompany him, carry out whatever he commanded and remain his friends and allies, no matter what.

When they had taken their leave with the utmost of grace and courtesy, Meriadoc, accompanying the daughter of the Emperor, began the journey as planned. They were joined, in addition, by twelve

autem eum xii comites ingenuitate et diviciis conspicui[1] procerumque multitudo usque ad lxxxiiii quos non minus xx milia militum sequebantur. Nam cum tanta militum copiositate advenit, ut eciam imperatori terribilis videretur. Adventanti autem imperator quasi gratulabundus occurrit, aliud vultu pretendens quam quod mente machinabatur. Jussit autem omnem turbam que cum eo venerat, exceptis primoribus, circumcirca per villulas et castella hospitari, volens, si quid accidisset, omne robur exercitus ab eo remocius consistere, quatinus eorum presencia ei minime foret presidio. Primores autem et principes cum Meriadoco (F. col. 2) in suo excepit palacio. Aggregaverat autem et imperator innumerabilem miliciam, ita ut vix urbis qua morabantur menia ipsam capere[n]t. Natam vero suam statim, ubi advenit, a consorcio Meriadoci removens,[2] in celsiori turre constituit, adhibita ei[3] diligenciori custodia. Ne tamen dolus pateret, aditus ad eam Meriadoco minime negabatur; sed quid inter eos gereretur suis sedulo rimari iussit, occasionem adversus eum querens qua iuste videretur eum gravare debere.

1   R. conspicium.
2   R. amovens.
3   R. illi.

high-born counts conspicuous for their wealth, and a number of noblemen, to the total of eighty-four, who were followed by no less than 20,000 knights. For Meriadoc came with such an enormous number of knights that he seemed to the Emperor even more formidable. On arrival, the Emperor rushed to meet him as if he would congratulate him, showing a face altogether different from the plotting of his mind. He ordered the entire force that had come with him, except for the ranking members, to be quartered in the little villages and small castles round about, desiring, if anything should happen, that with the strength of the entire army stationed at some distance from him, their presence would be of little support for him. The Emperor received the highest ranking men and princes, along with Meriadoc, in his palace. Meanwhile, the Emperor had assembled an uncounted number of his own knights, so many that the fortifications of his city in which they were quartered could scarcely hold them.

Separating his daughter from Meriadoc's party immediately after they had arrived, he placed her in the highest tower and set an extremely close watch over her. Nor was his deceit apparent. Meriadoc's access to her was not in the least denied; but what went on between them the Emperor ordered to be closely observed, seeking a pretext against him by which he would seem to accuse him justly.

Nunciatur imperatori interea ab insidiantibus, Meriadocum cum filia sua sepius secreta verba conserere, oscula inmoderacius imprimere et striccioribus stringere colla complexibus. Quod imperator audiens ad suam exercendam nequiciam se viam reperisse[1] congratulatus est[2] valde. Convocat igitur omnes principes qui ad curiam convenerant una cum Meriadoco et suis proceribus, induxitque palacio, quasi cum eis super aliquo consulataturus negocio. Universam[3] autem reliquam turbam clausis iussit amoveri foribus. Occuluerat[4] autem et infra palacium et extra in pomerium quo ab aquilonari parte ambiebatur palacium validam manum armatorum usque ad mille quingentos milites, quibus signum dederat, quid quando agere proposuerat. Facto igitur concessu nobilium et silencio imperato, "Nos vos," ait imperator, "O patres et principes, latere existime quo affectu meos fami(F. f. 21v)liares semper coluerim vel quibus honoribus mihi fideles[5] extulerim quantisve[6] sub me militantes sim solitus remunerari[7] stipendiis. Cum amicis mihi namque est secretorum communicacio, cum de me iam bene meritis regni tuicio, cum mihi

1 F. repperisse.
2 F. est *omitted.*
3 F. Universum.
4 R. Oocculerat.
5 R. fideles mihi.
6 R. quibusve.
7 R. remunerare.

The spies in a short time brought word to the Emperor that when Meriadoc was with his daughter, they frequently whispered words in secret and kissed one another passionately, and that he would embrace her tightly with his arms about her neck. So the Emperor, hearing that, knew he had found the way to perpetrate his evil plan, and he was filled with much joy. Therefore he called together all the nobles who had come to the court with Meriadoc and his own lords, and he led them into the palace as if he had some business or other to discuss with them. When the doors had been shut, he ordered all the rest of Meriadoc's party removed. Meanwhile he had hidden a strong contingent of armored men both within the palace and outside in the space next to the wall protecting the north side of the castle. To these 1,500 knights he had given a signal when they were to take the action he had planned.

When everything was in readiness, the permission of the nobles and their silence were requested. The Emperor spoke: "O patricians and princes, you I deem to be at my side as my inner circle. Vassals faithful to me, you I extoll with great honor. And ranks of knights under my banners, you I am accustomed to recompense with monetary reward. For it is my policy to share my secrets with my friends, the administration of the kingdom with those who merit it best, and the

militantibus thesaurorum particio. Illis diligentem, (R. p. 129) istis liberalem, reliquis[1] autem exhibere[2] munificum me semper studui. Hinc amicorum constanciam, procerum fidelitatem militum vero singularem circa me comparavi virtutem. Argumentum mee oracioni hic qui adest Meriadocus existit,[3] quem quam favorabiliter ad me adventantem exceperim, ad quante dignitatis gradus sublimaverim[4] satis habetur compertum. Primum namque ex stipendario in numero meorum familiarium eum accivi;[5] deinde gregariis universis et stipendariis militibus meis prefeci; auricularem et consiliarium meum constitui; preclaras illi quoque provincias ad regendum tradidi; hiisqui satis maiora ei conferre proposui, tum ob illius virtutem, tum quod id mee glorie rebar comparere, quidem strenuum[6] eum fateor multisque[7] pro me sudasse laboribus. Verumptamen queso cuius tociens triumphavit viribus? Nonne meis? Nonne robore[8] mei exercitus victor exstitit? Cuius est suffultus diviciis? Nonne suis ex meo erario stipendia prebebantur militibus? Duo quidem regna subegit. Sed quomodo? Decertante meo exercitu. Natam quoque meam de manibus Gundebaldi excussit. Sed

1 F. reliquiis.
2 F. aut exibire.
3 R. exstitit.
4 F. sullimaverim.
5 F. ascivi.
6 F. strennuum.
7 F. militisque.
8 F. corrobore.

portioning of my treasure to those who fight for me. I have always myself desired to confer my warmest esteem on those who advise me, liberal reward to those who serve me, and generous gifts to the rest. Thus I have gained the loyalty of friends, the fealty of noblemen, the incomparable prowess of knights in my court. The subject of my speech is Meriadoc and who precisely he actually is, he whom I have received coming before me with such acclamation, he whom I would have raised to a rank of great dignity had he been found worthy. For first I received him as a mercenary among my personal guard. Then I placed him in command over all my knights, both common soldiers and paid professionals. I made myself available both to listen and to advise; I handed over to him the richest provinces to bring about order. Of these I planned to confer the larger to him, not only on account of the prowess of the man, but also because I thought that this would display my honor. I admit that he sweated over certain rigorous tasks for me with much effort. Truly I ask, whose strength won the victory? Was it not mine? Is it not by my power that my army is triumphant? Whose wealth is the underlying support? Was it not from my gold that the wages were provided for his knights? He conquered two kingdoms. But how? By fighting it out using my army. He rescued my daughter from the hands of Gundebald. But by what means? By the plotting of my

per quid? Per industriam (F. col. 2) mee ipsius filie. Nichil ergo absque meo egit amminiculo. Ut tamen meam in eo liberalitatem et munificenciam ostenderem, super omnem quem ei ante honorem contuli, deliberavi meam copulare filiam, augere divicias insuper et terciam partem mei imperii eius subdere[1] dominio. Idque exequi iam festinassem, nisi scelus ipsius intervenisset quod me a meo divertit proposito. Tanto namque ipse Meriadocus in me excessit facinore, ut non solum[2] promissis[3] destitui beneficiis, verum eciam sit dignus dirissimis[4] subigi suppliciis. Meo quippe dedecori dedit operam nilque pudibundius quam quod gessit inferre potuit. Pudet me meimet[5] ipsius proferre verecundiam; nisi tamen proferatur a vobis, sciri non potest: filiam meam, quam me more regio[6] desponsaturum noverat, me insciente, oppressit, violavit, et, ut puto, sicut venter tumescens innuit, gravidam reliquit.[7] Meam munificenciam sua prevenit nequicia, illamque sibi prostituit que sibi illibata desponsare debuit. Apud vos igitur meam depono querelam, expectaturus quid vestra super hoc censura, equitate dictante, censeat."

1 R. subdere eius.
2 R. solum *omitted*.
3 F. promissus.
4 R. durissimis.
5 R. memet, me *omitted*.
6 R. regio sibi.
7 F. reliquid.

daughter herself. He has done nothing, therefore, without my assistance. For all that, I would have shown my liberality and munificence to him, conferred honor on him beyond all who preceded him, considered a marriage with my daughter, granting him enormous wealth and placing under his authority a third part of my empire. And this I would have already hastened to bring about, had a crime of this man not intervened, diverting my plan from what I had proposed. For so far has that Meriadoc transgressed against me in evil that not only have I withdrawn the rewards I had promised, but he may also deserve to undergo the direst punishment, on his knees disgraced before the executioner's axe. Indeed, he has shamed me willfully and nothing could be more shameful than what he has done. It shames me to speak of his shamefulness, but unless it is disclosed by you, it cannot be known: without my knowledge, he forced and violated my daughter whom he had known would have been betrothed to him by me as befits royalty. And, I believe, since the swelling of her belly shows it, he has left her pregnant. His crime is greater than my generosity. He has prostituted her for himself, a maiden who ought to have been betrothed untouched. Among you, therefore, I place my grievance, awaiting what your judgment concerning this case, as justice dictates, may advise as punishment."

Ad hec Meriadocus, ultra quam credi potest miratus[1] et ob inauditam prodicionem que sibi intentabatur ira fervescens, dum in medium prosilisset, ut ab illatis se excusaret calumpniis, confestim qui in latebris[2] erant, accepto signo, hinc et inde eruperunt[3] armati. Meriadocum cum sociis, strictis gladiis, circum (F. f. 22r) dederunt, circumdatos ut inermes ceperunt, captosque abducentes in arcem[4] fortissimam que confinis erat palacio sub arta incluserunt custodia. Eadem quoque tempestate destinavit imperator quatuor legiones per circumiacentes villulas ad Meradoci occupandum (R. p. 130) exercitum, dato precepto, ut Meriadoco faventes ergastulis manciparent, qui autem niterentur resistere gladiis cederentur. Ex quibus plurimi, prodicione comperta, fugam inierunt; quidam viriliter pungnantes interfecti sunt; reliqua multitudo usque ad xiii m[ilia] sese imperatori dederunt. Sparsim quippe per villas hospitati fuerant, unde leviter ab imperialibus, ut incauti et dispersi, occupati sunt. Imperatoris autem filia ubi qua fraude sit circumventus Meriadocus audivit, tam ingenti est absor[p]ta merore,[5] ut vix a propriis manibus abstineret, quin semet ipsam interficeret. Continuit tamen mentis ardorem, certa de

1 R. admiratus.
2 R. lateribus.
3 R. proruperunt.
4 F. artem.
5 F. merrore.

At this Meriadoc, stunned beyond belief and burning with wrath on account of the premeditated attack by which he had been accused without a hearing, leaped into the center of the chamber so that he might defend himself from the accusation brought forward. Immediately the armed guards who had been concealed, seeing this as the signal, sprang forward from every side. They surrounded Meriadoc and his companions with swords drawn. They captured the trapped men, who were unarmed, and took them prisoner, leading them off to the strongest prison near the palace and placing them under close watch.

At the same time, the Emperor ordered four battalions deployed throughout the surrounding small communities to force Meriadoc's army to surrender. As the orders had been given, they were to seize those favoring Meriadoc as prisoners, and those who attempted to resist would be forced to yield their swords. Most of these men, when they learned of the treachery, took flight; others, fighting bravely, were killed; the remaining ones surrendered to the Emperor, about 13,000 of them. Here and there throughout the farmsteads these men had been housed as guests, so that, being separated and off guard, the Emperor's forces had easily taken them prisoner.

futuris existens, quod Meriadocus, si posset evadere, vicem suis proditoribus recompensaret.

Vicesimo autem die quo hec gesta sunt rex Gallie cum magna nobilitate advenit, sibi pactam filiam imperatoris in uxorem ducturus. Verum ubi ad puelle ventum est colloquium remque secrecius et diligencius investigans, eam gravidam rex[1] deprehendisset, ilico, quasi hoc[2] in iniuriam suam factum fuisset, ipsius repudiavit connubium, se scortum[3] in coniugium abiurans umquam duc(F. col. 2)turum. Federa quoque que cum imperatore inierat sine dilacione abrupit, id in suum dedecus machinatur fuisse sepius inculcans. Nil tamen quod[4] ei iure belli abstulerat penitus restituere voluit, sed, fracta pacis condicione, bellique[5] renovato tumultu, passim imperatoris depredabatur provincias. E contra imperator, ubi de pace sibi spes excidit, congregat[6] et ipse non parvas tam pedestrium quam equestrium copias, furentique regi maturat occurrere. Certus ab utrisque dies certaminis indicitur, quo quis eorum adeptus fuisset victoriam alterius potiretur imperio.

1   R. rex *before* eam.
2   F. hoc *omitted*.
3   F. sortum, "c" *added above line*.
4   F. que.
5   F. abstulerat ... tumulto *repeated, marked to delete*.
6   R. cogregat.

When the daughter of the Emperor heard that Meriadoc had been overcome by such treachery, she was consumed by anguish so overpowering that she was scarcely able to control her own hands lest she kill herself. Still she held to the love in her heart, confident of the outcome, knowing that if Meriadoc could escape, he would take vengeance on his betrayers.

In twenty days, however, after all this had taken place, the King of Gaul arrived with his great nobles, ready to marry the daughter of the Emperor as he had agreed. Indeed when the delegation had come and the matter concerning the young woman had been investigated most discreetly and carefully, the King was apprised of her pregnancy. Right then and there, as if this matter had been arranged as a personal insult, he repudiated his marriage to her, swearing that he would never take a whore in matrimony.

The treaty that he had made with the Emperor he repudiated immediately, always insisting that this ploy was contrived to shame him. What is more, he refused to yield anything that he had seized for himself by right of battle, so once the conditions of peace had been broken, the violence of warfare was renewed, and he ravaged the provinces of the Emperor in every direction. On the other hand, the Emperor, when the hope of peace for himself had been cut off, called

Meriadocus interea prefati turri tenebatur inclusus. Verum propter bellorum eventus laxiori servabatur custodia. Imperator enim[1] facti penitens a vinculis immunem eum[2] esse preceperat, sperans animum eius se aliquo modo posse lenire. Dolebat enim graviter, quod prodicionis pro eo arguebatur crimine, virum quod[3] sibi utilem perdidisset, regemque nichilominus sibi[4] hostem existere. Postquam autem Meriadocus bellum parari cognovit, qualiter evadere posset apud se sedule deliberabat. Segregatus namque a sociis per se solus manebat. Quid[d]am autem insolitum machinatus est, sicut mens hominis, ubi magis artatur, magis artificiosa sepius invenitur. Quodam igitur ves(F. f. 22v)pertino tempore omnes pannos quos habebat, exceptis lineis, in frusta conscidit,[5] ipsasque scissuras ad instar funiculi ad invicem connexuit,[6] funemque longissimum ex conscissa[7] veste contexuit. Quem eciam trabe ligatum per quandam humiliorem fe(R. p. 131)nestram deorsum deposuit, per quem ipse ad terram confestim descendit. Deinde, ut specie canis excubias falleret, usque ad vallum manibus pedibusque

1 R. enim *omitted.*
2 R. eum immunem.
3 R. virumque
4 R. sibi nichilominus.
5 F. concidit.
6 F. funemque ... contexuit *added in margin.*
7 F. concissa.

together his forces—no smaller number of foot soldiers than mounted men—and marched swiftly to confront the furious king. By both sides a specific day for battle was fixed by which he who won victory over the other would gain mastery of the Empire.

Meriadoc, meanwhile, was held a prisoner in that tower. Actually, because of the renewal of warfare, he was no longer guarded as stringently. The Emperor, regretting what he had done, instructed that he was to be freed from his chains, hoping thus to lighten his animosity toward himself. The Emperor regretted sorely that he had accused him of this crime of treachery because by so doing he had lost a man valuable to him, while the King of Gaul remained his enemy still.

When Meriadoc learned that a battle was being planned, he carefully considered how he might be able to escape. He was kept alone, separated from his companions. He contrived an extraordinary plan, as the mind of a man under great constraint often devises greater stratagems. So, as night began to fall, he cut all the clothes he had into strips, except his linens, tied these strips together into a kind of cordage, and braided an extremely long rope from the cuttings of his garments. After the rope was secured to a beam, he dropped it down through a lower window, through which he dropped quickly to earth. Then, so that he

repebat. Quo sine aliquo impedimento transito, ad domum cuiusdam militis, qui in vicino degebat, sibique[1] erat familiarissimus, citissime tendebat. A quo quidem ubi quis esset agnitus honorificentiss[im]e susceptus est et omnibus refocillatus deliciis. Tribus autem diebus cum eo perhendinavit. Quarto vero locum certaminis peciit una cum suo hospite, qui eciam adinuenit sibi in armis et equis queque erant necessaria.

Pugne dies illuxerat, et a suis ducibus armis septus uterque in campum decertaturus producitur exercitus. Meriadocus in[2] prima fronte se regalibus latenter ingessit cohortibus. Nulla mora, distinctis et ordinatis aciebus, discurrunt[3] pedites; congrediuntur equites; clamor ad sidera tollitur; cominus eminusque pungnatur; curruunt passim vulnerati; nunc hac, nunc illac, victi victoresque pellunt et propelluntur. At Meriadocus, inter primos se semper agens, principem milicie imperatoris obvium habuit. (F. col. 2) Cum

---

1   F. sique, -bi- *added above line.*
2   R. vero in.
3   F. discurrint.

might escape the notice of the watchdogs, he crawled on hands and knees to the wall. Having climbed over without further trouble, he ran as fast as he could to the home of a particular knight who lived nearby and who had been one of his closest companions. When the man recognized who he was, Meriadoc was received with the utmost honor and refreshed with all kinds of good food. He stayed with him three days. Then on the fourth, he sought the place of the battle, with only his host, who had equipped him with armor, horse, and whatever else was necessary.

The day of combat dawned and each army, armed by its commanders, was led forward onto the field where, enclosed, they were to fight the decisive contest. In the first rank was Meriadoc, who had secretly joined the royal troops. Without delay, the foot soldiers formed up in battle order moved in from either side; the knights engaged the center, and the din carried to the stars; hand–to–hand and at spear-throwing distance they fought; wounded men had fallen everywhere. Now here, now there, conquerors and conquered pushed forward and were pushed back.

Then Meriadoc, always keeping himself to the fore, challenged the commander of the Emperor's knights.

quo congressus se in necem[1] medio campo prostravit ac eius equum abduxit. Post hunc cuidam duci qui primam conducebat aciem occurrit. Huic quoque sub cavo pectore ferrum recondit mortiferum, abducensque sonipedem illum in suo sanguine volutantem reliquit.[2] Tercium imperatoris nepotem, qui post eum imperaturus credebatur, furibundus excepit; nec meliori omine,[3] istum quippe cum equo in una deiectum congerie nece mulctavit[4] tristesque manes ad Tartara misit. Deinde orbiculatim inter utrasque perequitans acies, quasi imperialibus insultaret, splendidam in eos lanceam vibrabat atque ad suum lacessibat congressum.

Imperator autem,[5] ex interitu suorum optimatum et familiarium tanto accepto infortunio, animo nimis torquebatur, atque, nisi in eo vindicaretur, mori mallet quam vivere. Ignorabat tamen quis esset. Cumque illius congressum nullum suorum amplius conspiceret audere

---

1   F. semi necem.
2   F. reliquid.
3   F. homine.
4   F. *cancelling dot under* "c".
5   R. vero.

When the two met in the middle of the battlefield, he killed him and led away his horse. After this he attacked a certain duke who was leading the front rank. He buried the death-dealing lance into the hollow of his chest, and leading his horse away, left him rolling in his own blood. Third, he found the nephew of the Emperor, the man who it was believed would be the Emperor's heir; no better omen, he struck that one furiously and, along with his horse, dashed them to death in one heap. He sent his sad shade to Tartarus. Then, riding about in circles among the other battle-lines, as if he would challenge the whole imperial forces, he brandished his splendid lance at them and dared them to attack him.

The Emperor, however, when he had received the disastrous word of the deaths of his best and closest knights, was greatly tormented in mind. Unless he could vindicate them against that man, he preferred to die rather than to live. He did not know, moreover, who that man was. And since he perceived that none of his men would dare receive the blows of that man

excipere, "Occumbam," exclamavit, "cum ceteris, nisi hos qui occubuerunt ulciscar." Equum igitur calcaribus subducens ad cursum coegit Meriadocumque prefixa cuspide omni virtute peciit. E contra Meriadocus totis habenis in imperatorem admisit sonipedem atque in eum preceps irruit. Eoque imperatorem aggressus est impetu, ut nec clipeus obstiterit nec lorica, quin valida impacta dextra lancea ei penetralia transverberaret et cum (F. f. 23r) calido sanguine spiritum per auras eliceret. Dum autem corrueret, "Qualia," inquit[1] Meriadocus, "mihi, O imperator, prebuisti stipendia talia, et ego tibi impendo servicia." Hec dicens, se continuo catervis armatorum immiscuit, ne cui comperiretur quis esset (R. p. 132) evadere cupiens. Rex autem quecumque gesserat sedulo conte[m]platus lumine mittit statim post eum qui illum ad se cum honore deducerent, ne tam probus miles suam evaderet noticiam, et quia ipsius gestiebat remunerari virtutem qua de tam valido hoste triumphaverat. Cumque ante se ductus fuisset Meriadocumque cognovisset, cuius probitas sibi satis relata fuerat, rex subridens, "Meriadoce, Meriadoce," ait, "e[2] merito in illum talia exercuisti quem tante perfidie constat in te co[m]misisse facinus. Laborasti pro me, nec ero tibi ingratus, sicut ille exstitit. Ille tibi uxorem mei causa abstulit; ego vera illam restituam."

1   F. inquid.
2   R. e *omitted.*

any more, he screamed, "I will die with the rest if I cannot avenge the fallen." He pressed his spurs to his horse and began the charge. He sought Meriadoc with all his might, lance couched. Against him Meriadoc, loosing his reins completely, raced his horse toward the Emperor and met him headlong. He had attacked the Emperor with such a blow that neither shield nor mail could block it; with the lance impelled by the strength of his right arm, he pierced him through and, along with his warm blood, he released his spirit to the air. While he was sinking, Meriadoc shouted out, "O Emperor, of such quality are the wages you paid me, and I now pay you the same allowance." Having said this, he immediately rejoined the body of armored men, wishing to avoid anyone learning who he was.

But the King, who had observed in detail what had happened in the full light of day, quickly sent after him, ordering him led before him with honor, lest so skilled a knight should evade any recognition. He wanted very much to reward the courage of the man who had vanquished so strong an enemy. And when the knight had been brought before him and he recognized it was Meriadoc, whose prowess had been reported to him, the King, smiling at last, said, "You have requited that man as he deserved, the man who repaid you with such treachery for what he asked you to accomplish. You have now fought for me, nor will I be as ungracious as that man was. He took your

Neci igitur imperatore tradito, ipsius totus dispergitur exercitus. Verum non multum post regis Gallie dicioni cum universo imperio subditur. Rex autem, imperii potitus gubernaculo, Meriadoco confestim suam coniugem cum omnibus que ipse Meriadocus conquisi[v]erat restituit; insuper et magnas possessiones ei adiecit; suos proceres in custodia dententos[1] ei reddidit eumque secundum a se super totum suum imperium constituit. Nascitur post hec Meriadoco filius, ex quo multi reges et principes processerunt. Meriadocus vero in omni probitate consenuit.

Explicit[2]

---

1   F. decentos.
2   F. explicit *omitted*.

bride from you on my account. I therefore shall restore her to you."

Once the Emperor had been killed, all of his army was scattered. Indeed, not long after, the entire Empire was under the authority of the King of Gaul. The King, further, having been empowered with the government of the Empire, at once restored to Meriadoc his wife along with all the territory that Meriadoc had himself conquered. In addition he gave great estates to him, his companions held in prison he restored to him, and he established him as second only to himself over all his Empire. A son was born afterward to Meriadoc, from whom many kings and princes descended. Meriadoc, in truth, lived to the end of his days in all honor.

The End

The Garland Library
of Medieval Literature

Series A (Texts and Translations); Series B (Translations Only)

1. Chrétien de Troyes: *Lancelot*, or *The Knight of the Cart*. Edited and translated by William W. Kibler. Series A.
2. Brunetto Latini: *Il Tesoretto (The Little Treasure)*. Edited and translated by Julia Bolton Holloway. Series A.
3. *The Poetry of Arnaut Daniel*. Edited and translated by James J. Wilhelm. Series A.
4. *The Poetry of William VII, Count of Poitiers, IX Duke of Aquitaine*. Edited and translated by Gerald A. Bond; music edited by Hendrik van der Werf. Series A.
5. *The Poetry of Cercamon and Jaufre Rudel*. Edited and translated by George Wolf and Roy Rosenstein; music edited by Hendrik van der Werf. Series A.
6. *The Vidas of the Troubadours*. Translated by Margarita Egan. Series B.
7. *Medieval Latin Poems of Male Love and Friendship*. Translated by Thomas Stehling. Series A.
8. *Bartbar Saga*. Edited and translated by Jon Skaptason and Phillip Pulsiano. Series A.
9. Guillaume de Machaut: *Judgment of the King of Bohemia (Le Jugement dou Roy de Behaingne)*. Edited and translated by R. Barton Palmer. Series A.
10. *Three Lives of the Last Englishmen*. Translated by Michael Swanton. Series B.
11. Giovanni Boccaccio: *Eclogues*. Edited and translated by Janet Smarr. Series A.
12. Hartmann von Aue: *Erec*. Translated by Thomas L. Keller. Series B.
13. *Waltharius* and *Ruodlieb*. Edited and translated by Dennis M. Kratz. Series A.
14. *The Writings of Medieval Women*. Translated by Marcelle Thiébaux. Series B.
15. *The Rise of Gawain, Nephew of Arthur (De ortu Waluuanii Nepotis Arturi)*. Edited and translated by Mildred Leake Day. Series A.
16, 17. *The French Fabliau:* B.N. 837. Edited and translated by Raymond Eichmann and John DuVal. Series A.
18. *The Poetry of Guido Cavalcanti*. Edited and translated by Lowry Nelson, Jr. Series A.
19. Hartmann von Aue: *Iwein*. Edited and translated by Patrick M. McConeghy. Series A.
20. *Seven Medieval Latin Comedies*. Translated by Alison Goddard Elliott. Series B.
21. Christine de Pizan: *The Epistle of the Prison of Human Life*. Edited and translated by Josette A. Wisman. Series A.
22. *The Poetry of the Sicilian School*. Edited and translated by Frede Jensen. Series A.
23. *The Poetry of Cino da Pistoia*. Edited and translated by Christopher Kleinhenz. Series A.

24. *The Lyrics and Melodies of Adam de la Halle.* Lyrics edited and translated by Deborah Hubbard Nelson; music edited by Hendrik van der Werf. Series A.
25. Chrétien de Troyes: *Erec and Enide.* Edited and translated by Carleton W. Carroll. Series A.
26. *Three Ovidian Tales of Love.* Edited and translated by Raymond J. Cormier. Series A.
27. *The Poetry of Guido Guinizelli.* Edited and translated by Robert Edwards. Series A.
28. Wernher der Gartenaere: *Helmbrecht.* Edited by Ulrich Seelbach; introduced and translated by Linda B. Parshall. Series A.
29. *Pathelin and Other Farces.* Edited and translated by Richard Switzer and Mireille Guillet-Rydell. Series A.
30. *Les Cent Nouvelles Nouvelles.* Translated by Judith Bruskin Diner. Series B.
31. Gerald of Wales (Giraldus Cambrensis): *The Life of St. Hugh of Avalon.* Edited and translated by Richard M. Loomis. Series A.
32. *L'Art d'Amours (The Art of Love).* Translated by Lawrence Blonquist. Series B.
33. Giovanni Boccaccio: *L'Ameto.* Translated by Judith Serafini-Sauli. Series B.
34, 35. *The Medieval Pastourelle.* Selected, translated, and edited in part by William D. Paden, Jr. Series A.
36. Béroul: *Tristan.* Edited and translated by Norris J. Lacy. Series A.
37. *Graelent* and *Guingamor:* Two Breton Lays. Edited and translated by Russell Weingartner. Series A.
38. Heinrich von Veldeke: *Eneit.* Translated by J. Wesley Thomas. Series B.
39. *The Lyrics and Melodies of Gace Brulé.* Edited and translated by Samuel Rosenberg and Samuel Danon; music edited by Hendrik van der Werf. Series A.
40. Giovanni Boccaccio: *Life of Dante.* Edited and translated by Vincenzo Bollettino. Series A.
41. *The Lyrics of Thibaut de Champagne.* Edited and translated by Kathleen J. Brahney. Series A.
42. *The Poetry of Sordello.* Edited and translated by James J. Wilhelm. Series A.
43. Giovanni Boccaccio: *Il Filocolo.* Translated by Donald S. Cheney with the collaboration of Thomas G. Bergin. Series B.
44. *Le Roman de Thèbes (The Story of Thebes).* Translated by John Smartt Coley. Series B.
45. Guillaume de Machaut: *The Judgment of the King of Navarre (Le Jugement dou Roy de Navarre).* Translated and edited by R. Barton Palmer. Series A.
46. *The French Chansons of Charles D'Orléans.* With the Corresponding Middle English Chansons. Edited and translated by Sarah Spence. Series A.
47. *The Pilgrimage of Charlemagne* and *Aucassin and Nicolette.* Edited and translated by Glyn S. Burgess and Anne Elizabeth Cobby. Series A.
48. Chrétien de Troyes: *The Knight with the Lion,* or *Yvain.* Edited and translated by William W. Kibler. Series A.
49. *Carmina Burana.* Translated by Edward Blodgett and Roy Arthur Swanson. Series B.
50. *The Story of Meriadoc, King of Cambria (Historia Meriadoci, Regis Cambriae).* Edited and translated by Mildred Leake Day. Series A.
51. *Ysengrimus the Wolf.* Translated by Gillian Adams. Series B.

52. *Medieval Debate Poetry: Vernacular Works.* Edited and translated by Michel-André Bossy. Series A.
53. Giovanni Boccaccio: *Il Filostrato.* Translated by Robert P. apRoberts and Anna Bruni Seldis; Italian text by Vincenzo Pernicone. Series A.
54. Guillaume de Machaut: *La Fonteinne amoureuse.* Edited and translated by Brenda Hosington. Series A.
55. *The Knight of the Parrot (Le Chevalier du Papegau).* Translated by Thomas E. Vesce. Series B.
56. *The Saga of Thidrek of Bern (Thidrekssaga af Bern).* Translated by Edward R. Haymes. Series. B.
57. Wolfram von Eschenbach: *Titurel.* Edited and translated by Sidney M. Johnson and Marion Gibbs. Series A.
58. Der Stricker: *Daniel of the Blossoming Valley.* Translated by Michael Resler. Series B.
59. *The Byelorussian Tristan.* Translated by Zora Kipel. Series B.
60. *The Marvels of Rigomer.* Translated by Thomas E. Vesce. Series B.
61. *The Song of Aspremont (La Chanson d'Aspremont).* Translated by Michael A. Newth. Series B.

For Product Safety Concerns and Information please contact our EU representative GPSR@taylorandfrancis.com
Taylor & Francis Verlag GmbH, Kaufingerstraße 24, 80331 München, Germany

www.ingramcontent.com/pod-product-compliance
Lightning Source LLC
Chambersburg PA
CBHW071812300426
44116CB00009B/1286